CW00819430

Float Fishing

Beyond the basics

By
Richard Blackburn

ISBN: 978-1-8382478-3-6

Table of Contents

Foreword

As a youngster I learnt how to set my tackle, cast a line and land a fish, but there were things I just did not understand. Why did I blank so often? What were others doing that I wasn't? How can I find out? I remember being frustrated by the lack of books on float fishing much beyond the basics.

Despite giant leaps in information technology, it seems to me that little has changed, so I decided to write the book I always wanted to read and this is it.

I have not covered any of the basics. I assume you already know your knots and the difference between a Waggler and a stick. Instead I have reviewed some essentials and gone straight on to float fishing beyond the basics.

Best of luck, Richard.

Still Water

A float is able to describe exactly what's happening below the surface. For some it speaks with a loud voice, but in broken sentences. For others, every whisper is clearly heard, understood and interpreted. Novice anglers comprehend the clear language of the float being pulled under, but the gentle dialect of movements can be misunderstood. Of all the various techniques used in fishing, I believe the float to be the most deceptive. It appears a simple concept, but many an angler has sat patiently waiting for that clear signal which either never came or happened very infrequently. I imagine you have already had some success and would now like to go beyond the float shouting at you. Let's first look at some basic still water float rigs, to both confirm what you may already know and also as a starting point from which we can work.

Basic Loaded Waggler Rig

A loaded Waggler has much of it's shot carrying capacity built in, only the addition of a few split shots down the line are needed to finish a rig. The Waggler float itself is held in place on the line with a float stop on either side. The additional shots are then equally spaced down the line below the float. Finally, a hook link of a weaker breaking strain than the main line is added and Fig.1 is the result, a basic Waggler rig.

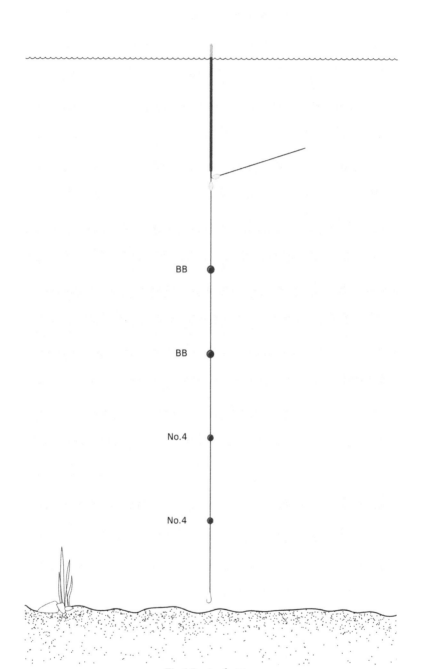

BB

BB

No.4

No.4

Fig.1 Basic shotting

Slide the rubber stops and float to set the depth at which the bait is to be presented to the fish. The strung out shotting pattern in Fig.1, efficiently gets the bait down to bottom where fish such as tench, bream, carp, roach and others can be caught. When a fish takes the bait, expect to see a classic bite with the float bobbing once or twice and then dipping below the surface, just as one might imagine.

Dip bites (where the float is pulled under) are easy to see and understand, but they rely on the fish swimming away with the bait in it's mouth. Some fish don't move away though, they stay put, prefering to eat the bait on the spot. For those fish, the angler must watch for a lift bite, a bite where the float rises (lifts) up in the water. This happens when a fish takes the bait off the bottom and lifts it's head to eat it (Fig.2). As the fish lifts it's head, the weight of the last shot nearest the hook, the tell tale, is also lifted. Because the weight of the tell tale is no longer pulling down on the float, the float is free to pop up a little indicating the presence of a fish. Fish don't always do one or other of these things, but it should be understood that a float will not move unless something makes it. Any unexpected movement should be regarded as a possible bite. Dips and lifts are the two most common indications, but sliding away, shaking and bobbing inexplicably could all be caused by a fish.

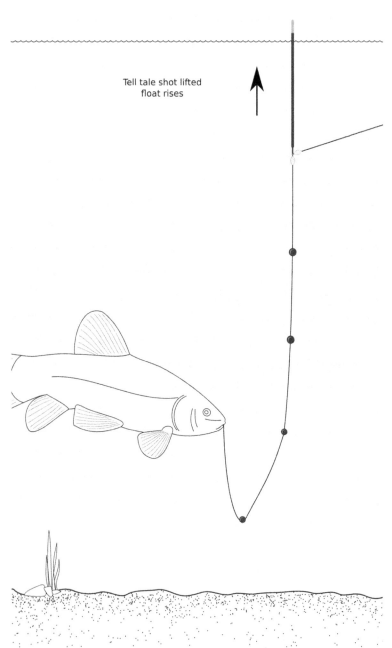

Tell tale shot lifted
float rises

Fig.2 Lift bite

Float Sensitivity

It's a common belief that a sensitive float is a light float and that sensitive floats catch more fish. Conversely, do not hesitate to use a heavy float when conditions call for it. These two views appear to be at odds. When talking of float float sensitivity, we are really only speaking about the buoyancy of the tip. Temporarily ignoring any other factors that may affect how a float behaves, let's think only about the tip. Imagine all the shots below the loaded Waggler shown in Fig.1 are removed. Without the balance of the shots down the line, a loaded Waggler might stand 4cm above the water. To cock the float correctly, an additional three BB shots are required. Each BB will pull the float down by 1cm, until all three pull together leaving 1cm of float tip above the surface.

If another BB was added, the float would sink below the surface. We could say that each centimetre of float has the buoyancy to support one BB. Or we could view it as a fish only needs to exert 0.4 grams of pull (the weight of one BB) to sink the float 1cm. To indicate a lift bite, the fish only needs to carry the weight of one BB to allow the float to pop up by 1cm. It should be remembered though, all other weights used in the rig are still being supported by the buoyancy in the rest of the float, only the 0.4g weight of a BB is required to sink or lift the float tip by 1cm.

Commonly, loaded Wagglers are made of clear hollow plastic. Their buoyancy comes from the air trapped inside them. A float of the same length, but twice as thick, would have twice the buoyancy. Two BB's would be needed to sink 1cm of tip and a fish would need to carry 0.8g to allow the float to pop up 1cm. We can deduce from this, that a more buoyant float needs extra effort to pull it under, or a fish has to carry more weight to cause it to pop up. If we go the other way and use a float of the same length, but half as thick, it follows the float would have half the buoyancy. Only 0.2g to sink the tip, or for the fish to carry 0.2g to cause a 1cm lift bite. The sensitivity of a float can be thought of as to how much buoyancy there is in the tip, depending on the density and thickness of the material used to construct the float.

Float sensitivity can be summed up as:

More buoyant - less sensitive.
Less buoyant - more sensitive.

A float that is half as thick may be a sensitive bite indicator, but because the whole float is thinner, it will carry less weight making it difficult to cast. So instead of making a Waggler out of one thin piece of tubing, a thin insert is pushed into the top of a normal Waggler. These Insert Wagglers have enough shot carrying capacity for casting, but are sensitive, because the tip is made of a thinner, less buoyant insert. The best of both worlds.

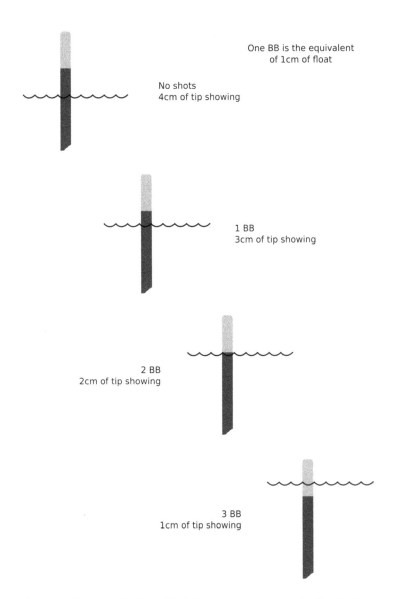

One BB is the equivalent
of 1cm of float

No shots
4cm of tip showing

1 BB
3cm of tip showing

2 BB
2cm of tip showing

3 BB
1cm of tip showing

To cock the float correctly, three BB shots are required, each one pulling the float down by 1cm,until all three pulling together leave 1cm of tip above the surface.

Fig.3 Float pulled down 1cm at a time by each BB

Fig.4 Insert Waggler

Insert Wagglers are extraordinarily popular with pleasure anglers, they solve both the sensitivity and casting weight problems in one. To take full advantage of an Insert Wagglers inherent sensitivity, a slightly different shotting pattern is called for. Because only a small amount of weight is needed to cause an indication, the tell tale shot need not be as big as the No.4 used in Fig.1. Depending on how buoyant the insert is, a No.6 or smaller could be used to get the same 1cm lift or dip bite mentioned earlier.

There are two common shotting patterns to use with an insert Waggler. Evenly spaced shot down the line with a No.6 as the tell tale, or a bulk of shots with a tell tale (Fig.5).

Bulking the shot together is used to get the bait down quickly past small nuisance fish near the surface and for greater stability in windy conditions. To reduce tangles on the cast, it's important to have a greater separation between the tell tale and the bulk, than between the tell tale and hook. Using the tell tale as a pivot point, the hook should not be able to reach the bulk when doubled back.

A strung out shotting pattern allows the bait to sink more slowly to the bottom. Some fish, I have in mind roach and rudd, are adept at intercepting the bait as it falls through the water. The rate of descent can be slowed still further to deliberately target midwater silvers with yet another pattern.

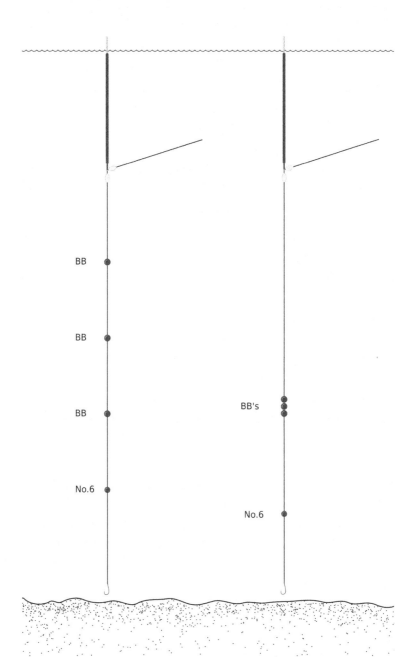

Fig.5 Insert Waggler shotting patterns

To give fish more time to intercept a falling bait, some of the weight is removed from down the line and grouped around the bottom of the float (Fig.6). Float stops are not needed as these shots hold the float in place, fix one shot above and the rest below the float. The remaining weight needed to cock the float, is broken down into no.8's or No.10's and evenly spaced down the line.

By reducing the amount of weight strung out down the line, the bait is presented differently, it sinks far more slowly. You might imagine choosing to put all the weight around the float leaving nothing on the line might enhance fishing on the drop, but there are two good reasons you should not. Firstly, the water resistance offered by the line must be overcome, not only surface tension, but also below the surface. Part of the deception is for your bait to fall as naturally as possible. A bait falling more slowly than any free offerings introduced, will raise suspicion among the older, bigger, wiser fish. Secondly, a line with no weight at all has a mind of it's own, it can go into coils, become tangled and knotted. Adding dust shots even as small as No.10's go a long way to control the line. Main line of 1 or 2 lb breaking strain is ideal and more than strong enough to handle roach and rudd. On the subject of line, Monofilament is my preference, not just on the drop, but for all my float fishing. The important property of Mono is the fact that it absorbs water. After perhaps 15 minutes, Mono absorbs enough to become neutrally buoyant, a distinct advantage when float fishing.

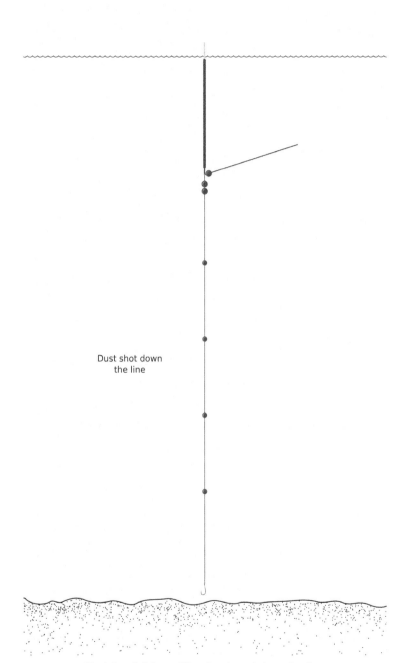

Dust shot down
the line

Fig.6 Loaded Insert Waggler slow sink on the drop

Silvers in particular spend much of their time opportunistically feeding in mid water, causing the bait to sink naturally will help to catch them. Extremes of temperature are often a clue as to whether or not to fish on the drop. On a hot summer's day, rudd may be the only species that will feed. In the depths of winter, on a day when you can see your breath and all the colour has dropped out of the lake, fishing on the drop for Roach can be very rewarding.

When fishing fine in extremes of temperature, one must accept the possibility of losing the odd bigger fish in return for using a method that will catch dozens of silvers. I believe it's better to balance the tackle to ensure a steady stream of fish through the day rather than the off chance of catching one or two reasonable fish.

The lake bed is where most anglers like to present their bait and for good reason. All course fish will pick food up off the bottom and for many, the lake bed is their larder. Tench, bream, skimmers, roach and carp are the likely species sought by still water float anglers. These fish are very adept at finding food on the lake bed, although at times even midwater fish like rudd can be caught there. Fishing on the bottom can mean offering a hook bait laying hard on the bottom, just touching bottom or just held above the bottom. There are a number of variables that can help decide which presentation to use. Fish behaviour, type of lake bed and weather conditions being the most important. All three of these factors have to be considered individually and together.

For the moment I am going to concentrate on factors other than the type of fish, starting with the lake bed.

Wherever you fish, use common sense and observation to build a picture of the lake bed. If the lake is well established and surrounded by trees, suspect a silt bottom. If it's a commercial dug for the purpose, suspect a clear, flat bottom. Without diving to look, the best method of deciding what the bottom is like, is to cast out and drag a small bomb across the lake bed to feel for yourself what's there. Use a fairly stiff rod and braid to feel every detail of the bottom even at distance.

Once you have an idea of the type of bottom you are fishing over, plumb the depth in the areas of interest and set your rig accordingly. Usually I start with the depth set to cause the bait to just touch the bottom, not always easy on a layer of deep silt or a bottom covered in debris and leaf litter. This initial depth is quite arbitrary, as you will almost certainly have to change it. Let's assume conditions allow the use of an insert Waggler as illustrated in Fig.6, strung out shot with a No.6 tell tale. Let's further assume the lake is a mixed fishery with all the common species. For the moment we will not concern ourselves with baits and hooks, just the mechanics of presentation and bite registration.

The position of the tell tale has a big influence on how clearly bites are indicated. Unfortunately catching a few fish is the only way to know how well the setup is working, which can be frustrating as getting a bite may require the rig to be adjusted in the first place.

An insert Waggler is able to indicate both dip and lift bites. By watching how the float behaves and how well the fish are hooked, it is possible to make adjustments to optimise the presentation and bite registration. With the bait just touching bottom and the tell tale shot eight inches from the hook, a fish will cause a dip bite if it takes the bait and swims off along the bottom. I prefer the sudden dip of my float not to be a surprise, ideally I want some warning by the float bobbing up and down once or twice before the fish swims away pulling it under. Pulling on the line or disturbing the tell tale shot are what we want reported at the float. If the tell tale was some distance from the hook, there would be more line between it and the hook. A fish could take the bait and swim further before the tell tale was disturbed, this in effect gives the fish more room to move before any indication. The fish could take the bait and remain stationary long enough to eat the bait and reject the hook, all without any indication at the float. The further away the tell tale shot is from the hook, the less sensitive the rig. Giving the fish enough rope to hang themselves doesn't always work. Conversely, having the tell tale very close to the hook has the opposite effect, the fish barely has to touch the bait to cause an indication. The problem then becomes, the fish hasn't got the bait properly in it's mouth before you strike, resulting in many missed fish.

The best way of determining the position of the tell tale shot, is by observing the floats behaviour and where in the mouth the fish is hooked. If hooked just in the lip, the tell tale is too close to the hook. In other words, the rig is so sensitive it's indicating a bite too soon and before the bait is fully in the fish's mouth. If fish are deeply hooked needing the use of a disgorger, then consider moving the tell tale closer. Over the capture of a few fish, the optimum position of the tell tale can be determined. It should be close enough to cause a few warning bobs as the fish mouths the bait, but then lifts or dips positively. Upon landing, the hook should be found just inside the mouth. Needless to say, if different sizes or species of fish move into your swim, re-evaluate and adjust the position of the tell tale as necessary.

All fish are capable of taking a bait presented at dead depth, but some are better at it than others. Strange bites and foul hooked fish may show a dead depth presentation is less than ideal for the fish in your swim. Tench, bream and Crucians in particular use a technique whereby they tilt their bodies down, sometimes to a point where they are vertical, to suck up material on or very near the bottom. But most fish have monocular vision, making it impossible for them to see anything directly in front. As they pitch their heads down to a bait at dead depth, the actions of their pectoral and pelvic fins can cause the bait to move, preventing them from picking it up. Not only that, but their forehead or back may touch the line and push the bait out of reach, in either event the bait will move from where the fish expected to find it. On the surface, the float will bob about, or display an unnatural sideways movement. If you strike at these strange indications and manage to hook something, the fish will almost certainly be foul hooked just outside the mouth or under the chin.

Faced with this evidence, a better approach may be to fish over depth laying some line on the bottom. Over depth can mean anything from an inch to a foot of line on the lake bed, although four inches is a good place to start. Move all the components of the rig up the line by the amount of line to be laid on the bottom. The tell tale shot should maintain the same relation to the bottom as it did before moving to an over depth presentation. It may seem counterintuitive to have so much line between hook and tell tale. In practise though, any movement of the hook in any direction except directly towards the line hanging down from the float, will cause an indication at the surface. As before, observe the float, note where the fish are hooked and adjust the tell tale accordingly to get the best hook holds.

The third common presentation is to offer the bait under depth. This is a presentation many anglers find difficult to accept, the thought that a fish will take a bait suspended above the bottom. Yet underwater filming has revealed that fish readily take food stirred up off the bottom, as well as free offerings falling through the water. Fish will take a bait presented off the bottom if that is what they want at the time. The slow sinking rig in Fig.6 is the usual rig of choice set to stop short of the lake bed.

Deciding which presentation to use, is a decision that has to be made on the day. This decision can only be made by assessing the nature of the lake bed, knowing the species of fish you are likely to catch, observing how the float behaves and seeing where in the fish's mouth the hook is holding. A good angler is always actively fishing, never just waiting in expectation.

Conditions

Strong wind is perhaps weather a float angler like the least, not only for casting, but also because of float drift. A bait which is being pulled along the lake bed by a float that is itself being pushed by the wind looks most unnatural. Preventing a float and bait drifting out of the swim will simply allow a better presentation and more control. When the wind blows constantly in one direction for a time. The surface of the water moves with the wind towards one side of the lake. On reaching the windward bank, the water has to go somewhere. It cannot get over, so it will go down or to the side. Eventually a wind powered circulation begins within the lake, some areas will have quite a flow whereas others will be quite still. A shallow lake I know, often has water going in one direction down one bank and in the opposite direction on the other. The flow down the sides can reach a slow walking speed, fishing either of these banks is usually a waste of time. But, fishing at the end of the lake, where the water is headed, can produce a good day's fishing. Lake fish don't like flow. Compared to river fish they are weak and flabby and much prefer to avoid any effort. Nevertheless they know that any food suspended in the moving water will drop out as the water slows and turns at the ends of the lake. These slow areas are not only good for the fish, they are good for float fishing as any flow in the water is slower. Casting into the wind can also make presentation easier. In this position the main line is parallel to the wind direction greatly reducing it's effect. Given a choice, I prefer to fish the slack at the windward end of the lake, supporting the long held belief, it's better to fish with the wind in your face. In a deeper lake, the water may not circulate as if stirred by a giant spoon. Instead, when reaching the windward side, the water will go down rather than to the sides. In this instance the water will travel across the surface pushed by the wind in one direction, then return in the opposite direction along a deeper layer causing an undertow. Conversely, in a cold North or Easterly wind it is usually better to fish on the leeward side of a lake. I imagine the cooling of the water at the windward end does not suit the fish.

Snow fall, hail or cold rain will also affect the fish. Any cold water suddenly entering the lake will sink to the bottom often pushing the fish up in the water. Changing to fishing on the drop might be the only choice at that time. Surface drift in the wind is perhaps not so much of a problem because of the constant recasting, although I still prefer to sink the line on a windy day.

Combatting the wind

On some days the wind seems to come from all directions, it puffs and blusters causing ripples in patches and comes and goes without warning. It delights in gusting just as you ping out some maggots causing them to scatter in all directions. On other days, a steady wind will cause a definite flow in the water, when more effort is required to prevent the float and bait drifting out of the swim. In a steady wind most of the drift occurs in the upper layer of water. Sinking the line to a heavier, longer float and bulking some shots low on the line (Fig.5) to concentrate weight in a slower moving layer helps to control a float's drift. In the event this is not enough, a bait presented over depth with a few inches of line laying on the bottom to act as a brake, will steady a float in a light drift.

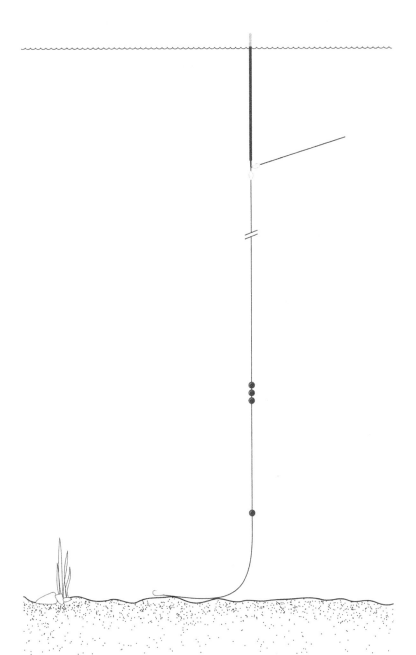

Fig.7 Waggler over depth in drift

To summarize our thoughts so far, it's important for the hook bait to look and behave as naturally as possible. It should either sink slowly, or remain stationary on or near the lake bed. Wind and rain will affect fish location and bait presentation, subjects which are instrumental in having a good day.

Unloaded Wagglers

One of the biggest bugbears with loaded floats is not being able to use any of the weight tied up in the loading. An unloaded float allows maximum flexibility in shotting patterns and weight distribution. As the name suggests, an unloaded Waggler is a float that does not have any of it's weight carrying capacity built into the float. Instead, shots are grouped around the base of the float to act as the main loading. One problem you may encounter with the larger non toxic shots in use today, is that they don't always close tightly around fine lines. To stop any movement when casting or striking, put a No.8 on either side to hold everything in place.

To avoid any repetition, you can safely assume rigs already described under the heading of loaded Wagglers are identical with an unloaded version, except for how the float is loaded. Instead let's continue with further examples of float control on windy days.

It's easy to assume that only the float is influenced by wind and water circulation, after all it's the float we see moving. In fact everything in the water from rod tip to hook is affected. Fishing line is very thin, yet the combined force of water pushing against the entire length of submerged line adds up.

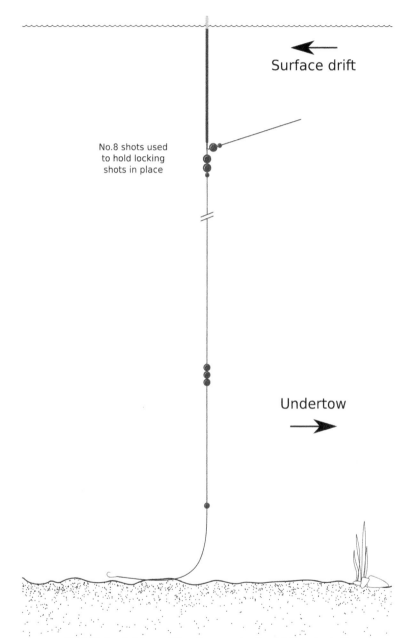

Surface drift

No.8 shots used
to hold locking
shots in place

Undertow

Fig.8 Unloaded insert Waggler over depth with heavier bulk

Surface Drift

No.8 or No.6
anchor shot

Fig.9 Anchor shot holding against drift

In a strong surface skim or an undertow (Fig.8), bulking shot in a lower layer may not be enough to stop the rig drifting. In addition to setting the rig over depth, an anchor shot can be added to the hook link to hold the rig in place (Fig.9).

After casting in and sinking the line, there will be a minute or two where the line is pushed by the water movement into a slight bow between rod tip and float. The flow also pushes against the float itself and the few feet of line down to the lake bed. A bow will form in the line and the float will be pulled until the anchor shot is reached. At this point with both ends of the line fixed, the float is the only part that can still move and if the flow is strong enough, the float will pull under out of sight. The reason is that there is not enough buoyancy in the tip to hold it up. You may remember that one No.6 shot is enough to sink an insert Waggler 1cm. If the force exerted over yards of sunken line by the wind driven circulation is enough to push with more force than the weight of a No.6, it will pull the float down in the water, if not sink it completely. Needless to say, the more sensitive a float tip, the less force needed and the more susceptible it is to movement in the water.

Surface Drift

Fig.10 Unloaded insert Waggler with tell tale as anchor

There are two ways to alleviate this sinking problem. First is to remove the anchor shot and adjust the rig until the tell tale is resting on the bottom (Fig.10). Because the tell tale is no longer pulling the float down it will pop up and sit higher above the surface. However, the float will be pulled down again by the force of the flow acting on the line cocking it correctly. This is quite a neat solution, it not only keeps the float visible, but also greatly exaggerates lift bites. A fish dislodging the tell tale from the bottom, will allow the float to suddenly pop up. What we have done is to balance the force of the flow acting on every part of the rig, with the buoyancy of the tip. Balancing the rig allows the use of a sensitive insert Waggler in conditions that are not ideal. However, windy days make ripples, and ripples can make the thin insert difficult to see. Squinting to see the float gives me a headache, so if ripples become a problem, I change the float.

My second solution to the sinking float problem when using an anchor shot, is to use a float with a more buoyant tip. Changing from an insert Waggler to a straight Waggler is the easiest way around the problem. Straight Wagglers are perhaps twice as buoyant making them much better at resisting any flow. They are also easier to see, so no headaches. Lift bites won't be as obvious, but against a rippled surface, I can live with that. On the subject of visibility, the colour of the tip has a bearing. Orange is a good colour in most conditions and on rippled water. White or bright yellow are good under trees and in dark areas. Black is ideal silhouetted against bright reflections, along with a pair of polaroid sunglasses.

When confronted with a surface skim and undertow, it's a matter of balancing the forces involved. However, when trying to offer a static bait on the lake bed in water of more than six feet deep, a problem arises whereby the locking shot around the float and the bulk can be separated by several feet of line. Trying to cast with these two weights so far apart, can result in more tangles. The best solution I've found is to create two bulks down the line. The first bulk is placed just below half depth, with a second bulk one third to halfway between the first bulk and the hook. Below the lower bulk will go the tell tale, it's final position determined by how the fish are responding. Having the shot more evenly distributed down the line makes casting less troublesome.

To help further with casting and presentation, there should be a progressive increase in weights from hook to float. For example (Fig.11), starting with one No.6 as the tell tale. Then above a bulk of two No.4's followed by a bulk of three N.o4's at half depth. Finally three AAA as float locking shots. Casting a deep water rig that may be six, eight or ten feet long is no easy task. Be aware of any hazards behind you, cast smoothly and with purpose. Fully follow through and feather the line down. Wait for the bulks to get down in the water before sinking the line and don't be afraid to use the longest, heaviest Waggler you have. Remember it's the tell tale and or first bulk which causes a bite. If the rig is working correctly, you should have hooked the fish long before it detects the heavy locking shots.

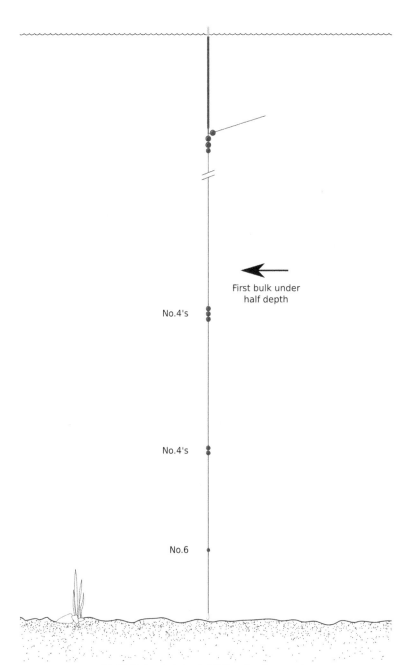

First bulk under
half depth

No.4's

No.4's

No.6

Fig.11 Unloaded straight Waggler deep water

It can be difficult to decide if the swim has an undertow before your float is in the water. Surface movement can be noticed by a few minutes of careful observation and an undertow may be suspected with prior knowledge of the lake and it's depth. Ultimately watching how the float behaves is the truest indicator, namely, if the float drifts against the wind, undertow is present. It is remarkable to see a float drifting against the wind, a most unnatural sight, yet perfectly understandable in the presence of undertow. Often if an undertow is strong enough to cause this phenomenon, employing an anchor shot, or resting the tell tale on the bottom is the only way to present a static bait hard on the lake bed.

Although dogma suggests a static bait hard on the bottom is always better, the environment hidden from us close to a lake bed may make this impossible. If the lake bed is silt, or has a mat of silkweed, then fishing dead depth or under depth is more likely to work. Keeping the bait still will be impossible, although this may not matter. If the fish are feeding above the bottom, they will likely expect any suspended matter to drift in the undertow. Under these circumstances, allowing the float to drift "downstream", may prove to be what the fish want and expect.

It is a challenge fishing in difficult conditions, it can be quite rewarding to successfully catch on such a day. On the occasions I have fished a difficult day, I have found myself fishing alone. Most sensible people go fishing to enjoy catching a few fish in fine weather, not battle the elements for every bite.

Hook links

I have always favoured using a weaker hook link which I expect to break before the main line if a fish overpowers the setup. Ready tied hook links are ideal and can be quickly changed to different line strength or hook size. Most ready made hook links are around 12" long with a loop tied in the end. A simple loop to loop connection is used to attach them to the main line. Ready tied hook links are very useful, but restrict you to the combination of line strengths to hook size you have brought along. Tying your own custom hook links to suit the method or conditions you are faced with may be tiresome, but ultimately pays off with more fish caught.

For me there are two fundamental types of hook link, short and long. My short links I tie in a way to cause the tell tale shot to rest on the knot 6" (15cm) from the hook. If I decide to use a loop to loop connection, I make the link about 5½" long allowing the tell tale to be 6" from the hook accounting for the two loops. If I'm using a figure-of-eight knot, then I simply tie the hook link on at 6" from the hook. A six inch hook link is, I find, a good length for targeting the common bottom feeding species such as carp and tench. The ability to register both dip and lift bites is essential when targeting these fish. To ensure a lift bite that is clear, a No.6 (or heavier) tell tale shot will be required. Shots of this size are undesirable on the hook link. Using a short hook link keeps the tell tale on the stronger main line, yet close enough to the bait to register a lift bite, but can be slid up the line if the fish or conditions call for it. On the whole I use short hook links, perhaps as short as 4", when fishing for bottom feeding species or in rough conditions when heavier gear may be needed.

At the other end of the scale, long hook links suit light rigs and tackle used to catch roach and other silvers. A long hook link made of fine line will allow the bait to behave more naturally. Only soft lead dust shots from No.8 and smaller are used to control the bait. Attaching shots to a fine hook link is best done before tying the link to the main line. Squeeze the required shot onto the end of the hook link and slide them up the line into position. Cut off and discard the damaged end before tying on the hook and tying the link to the main line with a figure-of-eight knot.

Whichever hook link I use, I like to make a good progression from hook link to main line by using a main line that is no more than 2lb stronger, with 1lb being preferred. Short hook links in particular look wrong to me when connected to a much thicker, stiffer main line. Although a fish may only see or feel the hook link, I feel continuity from hook link to main line is one of those small details that help to make a positive difference.

Most baits common to float fishing are soft and can be mounted directly on the hook. One popular exception to this are hard pellets. Ready tied banded hook links are available for silvers and float fishing. An alternative method is to push the hook through the wall of a latex band, then band the pellet in the usual way. The band can be removed at any time to switch back to a soft hook bait without the need to change the hook.

Fig.12 Banded pellet

Bodied Wagglers

Swinger floats

Despite the universal popularity of straight and insert Wagglers, I feel it's worth mentioning bodied Wagglers. Swingers can be imagined as a straight Waggler, but with a cork, balsa or polystyrene body, glued in place just above the eye. With it's extra buoyancy, a Swinger can carry much more weight than a straight Waggler allowing it to be cast further. For many anglers this is as far as their thoughts go, ignoring some important properties Swingers have. I don't propose to go through all the different bodied Wagglers there are. However, I will explain the useful properties and in certain circumstances, the benefits of bodied Wagglers leaving you to decide which are the most useful in the waters you fish.

A straight Waggler has it's buoyancy evenly distributed along the length of the float, and to my mind, an insert Waggler is little different. The body of a Swinger is positioned close to the bottom of the float, which has the effect of moving and concentrating much of the buoyancy down in the water. Accepting that, length for length, a bodied Waggler has a greater shot carrying capacity, how else does concentrating the buoyancy lower in the water help?

In heavy ripples, the evenly distributed buoyancy of a straight Waggler encourages the float to ride the waves causing the float to bob up and down, whereas a bodied Waggler with most of it's buoyancy safely well away from the surface is more stable.

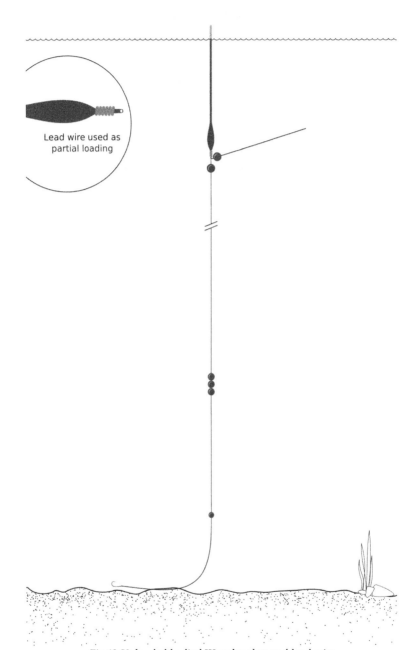

Lead wire used as partial loading

Fig.13 Unloaded bodied Waggler shot and lead wire

Fishing a large windswept water, or a river in a downstream wind, are two examples of when a bodied Waggler will out fish a straight. Tip buoyancy might be the same for similar straight and bodied Wagglers, but having extra buoyancy beneath the surface helps reduce the effects of surface skim helping with a static presentation. Unloaded swingers are more flexible in their shotting, but have a unique problem in that some shotting patterns end up with several big shots grouped around the float. To streamline these rigs, take an unloaded Swinger and wrap and glue lead wire to the end to add a custom amount of loading. Needless to say, any conventional float can be part loaded in this way.

If the body of a bodied Waggler bears most of the shot carrying capacity, then the shaft can be made in different lengths, or of different materials to suit almost any condition. This gives rise to many designs of specialist floats used in very defined conditions down to a granular level. Go down this route and you will quickly find you own dozens of floats which you hardly ever use. Although there is one special float I would recommend, the Driftbeater.

Driftbeater float

As the name suggests, the Driftbeater is the ultimate float for combating drift and undertow. As a special, it breaks many of the usual Waggler rules and should be regarded as separate from other floats attached by the bottom end. It does however, mash together several of the principals covered thus far. The Driftbeater is a bodied Waggler with a very thin shaft called an antenna. It has a bright sight bob allowing it to be seen at a distance and in choppy conditions. All of the float buoyancy is in the body, there is virtually no buoyancy in the antenna. The sight bob has an amount of buoyancy which holds it at the surface, but also makes bites easier to see.

Thinking about what we already know on float design. It is clear that because the shaft of the float has virtually no buoyancy, it will readily indicate a lift bite, even if only a small amount of weight is lifted by a fish. To resist both drift and undertow, the float employs three important principles, an anchor shot, bulk shot low in the water and nearly all of it's buoyancy below the surface.

All the Wagglers we have looked at so far have two thirds to three quarters of the total shot carrying capacity grouped around the float as locking shot. The Driftbeater is fixed in position with a one small shot on either side. A bulk of no more than four shots is used down the line of sufficient weight to cock the float except for the antenna, which should be completely sticking out of the water at this point.

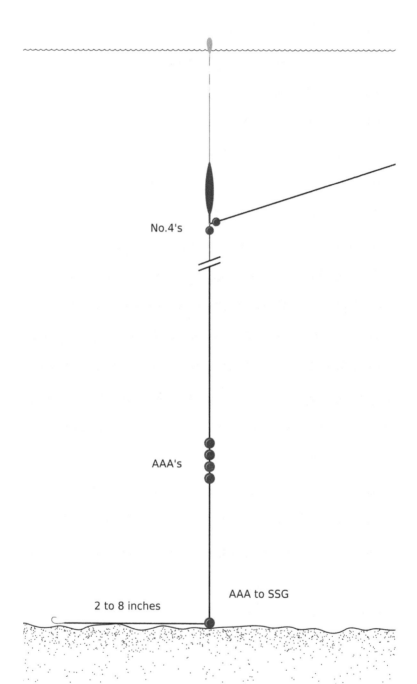

No.4's

AAA's

2 to 8 inches

AAA to SSG

Fig.14 Driftbeater rig

A single anchor shot is then added four inches from the hook, which is enough to sink the antenna and hold the rig static on the lake bed. Set the float to fish a couple of inches over depth to ensure the anchor is hard on the bottom. Cast the float out using a side or under arm cast, sink the line and place the rod in it's rests. Tighten up until the float pulls down to leave just the sight bob at the surface.

The size of the anchor shot is decided by the strength of surface flow and or undertow. The worse the conditions and the stronger the tow, the heavier the shot. Balancing the shot to the conditions makes the weight of the shot almost undetectable to the fish. Any movement of the anchor shot is immediately reported at the sight bob. The Driftbeater is closely associated with tench fishing, although it's only the bigger fish that cause a lift bite, juvenile tench seem to rush in, grab the bait and tear off causing a dip bite. Despite this close association with tench, the Driftbeater should be regarded as a tool for combating strong drift, the lift method proper, is a very old method employing a simple straight float.

If one was to pull off the Driftbeaters sight bob and use a Waggler shotting pattern, it would behave like an antenna float. It would be very sensitive in both lift and dip bites because of the negligible buoyancy in the tip, but would also become very susceptible to being pulled under in any strength of flow. Understanding float design and how a shotting pattern interacts will stand you in good stead when deciding what float to use at any particular time. There are very few circumstances, once the angler knows how floats and shotting patterns work, where a decision cannot be made, even if that decision is to ledger. I encourage you to be cautious of articles that contain the words "always" and "never". Ignore people who claim to be certain. Instead always, evaluate, experiment and adapt, but most of all, keep an open mind and be observant.

Slider float

The slider is a loaded float made from peacock quill with a high density foam body capable of carrying at least 2SSG. Used in depths of over 10ft where a fixed Waggler float would be impractical, a slider float allows line to pass through the bottom ring until the correct depth is reached at a stop knot. More than any other species, bream are associated with a slider rig. They often feed in deeper water and their bites are perhaps the easiest to hit on the strike with so much line out. I will describe a positive rig that rarely tangles and has recently become my favourite.

Thread the float on the line and attach a 6 inch hook link. Add a bulk of shots 36 inches above the hook. Small trimming shots are added directly under this bulk for fine tuning. A second small bulk of four or five No.8 or No.6 are placed from 6 to 12 inches above the hook. This second bulk acts as the tell tale and can be adjusted by moving the trimming shots down making the rig more positive, or sliding them back to make the rig more negative.

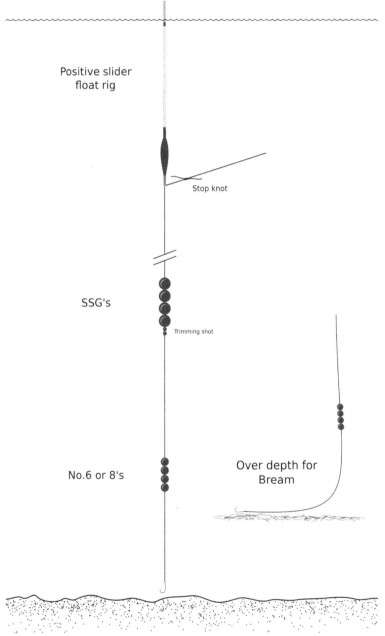

Positive slider
float rig

Stop knot

SSG's

Trimming shot

No.6 or 8's

Over depth for
Bream

Fig.15 Slider float rig

A stop knot is tied to the main line to stop the float at the correct depth. The stop knot is a simple four turn overhand knot tied from an off-cut of whatever main line is used. Leave long tail ends of two or three inches otherwise the knot will catch on the rod rings when casting. Depending on the size of the float eye, some anglers use a small glass bead between float and stop knot.

Fig.16 Stop knot

The float will rest against the large bulk on the cast. Despite not being fixed to the line, the float will remain very close to the bulk during flight staying together reducing tangles. Sink the line by submerging the rod tip and reeling in quickly to drag the line under. When the line is sunk and the float arrives over the feed, open the bail arm and allow the line to peel off the spool as the heavy bulk sinks. A sweeping vertical strike with a long rod is the most effective way to hook a fish in deep water.

A Time and Place

Recently I was fishing one of my favorite lakes and from my peg I could hear the metallic click of the entrance gate as it closed. Every time the gate clicked I found myself looking down the lake to see who came in. A few seconds later, a figure would pause at the water's edge to look at the lake before moving to a swim. What struck me was that all of them, without exception, spent no more than a few seconds surveying the lake before moving to a peg. Some dumped their gear in a peg close to the entrance, while others walked further round, but as far as I could tell, all went straight to a peg. It could be that all these anglers were experts, or that they knew the water so well that they only needed a few seconds to weigh the possibilities. I suspect though, most headed for a swim they were already familiar with, a swim they had caught at before. Alternatively, they have chosen to think like a match angler and trust the luck of the draw and try to catch whatever's in front of them.

Time is limited for the angler who has perhaps only one afternoon a week to fish, which may explain why so many people go to what they know. There's nothing wrong with fishing a favorite peg in the summer, when the fish are more active and spread throughout the lake, but things start to go wrong during unseasonal weather or at a different time of year. In the winter, fish will shoal together in the most comfortable part of the lake, leaving areas devoid of life that were teaming in the summer. Coming away with a blank is more likely, unless you take the time to get to know a fishery, how the fish behave and where they are at different times of the year.

When the gate clicks shut behind you and you take a first look at the lake, you may be drawn to the first peg you find near the entrance. Oddly this could well be one of the best pegs on the lake. Not because the entrance gate was carefully placed close to this remarkable swim, but because people don't want to carry their gear any further than they have to. A peg near the entrance is usually popular and the fish quickly learn that this part of the lake is rich in food.

It's common knowledge that fish are attracted to islands and weed beds, convenient swims near these features also become very popular. Even if the venue is new to you, the worn bank of a popular swim is a dead give away, although thought should be given as to why a particular peg is frequented more than others. A popular peg for the Method feeder for example, may not be any use to a float fisherman.

If competitions are fished, the productive pegs can be identified from the results. A look on the fisheries website will indicate hot pegs, information that might otherwise take many trips to learn. Competitions are fished throughout the year which will also reveal the seasonal preferences of the fish. Remember though, match angling is a specialised branch of the sport, in which carp are the main target species. While on the fishery website, have a look at the gallery of catch photos, these too can yield useful information. It may seem an oversimplification to suggest a look at a website or fish swims with worn banks, but on a busy fishery, you can't get away from the fact that swims where most fish are caught do have worn banks and a fishery website does yield useful information, so use them.

Worn banks and websites are a good starting point, but they are no substitute for really getting to know a place. Take a day to plumb the depths around the lake, accuracy is not important, but knowing the average depth and finding the shallows and any holes is. Take a camera, make notes, talk to people, build a picture of the lake. Make a rough sketch and mark the location and size of features like islands and reed beds. Is it an inline lake, is it natural or dug, what species of fish live there, do trees overhang the lake, is it in a valley or is it open and wind swept. Look on a map to see the lakes orientation, remembering the prevailing wind direction, which is westerly in the UK. Gain as much information as you can before dragging all your gear to the water's edge.

Concentrate your attention to areas within twenty five yards of the bank. Although it is possible to float fish further out, it gets very difficult. Casting might not be a problem on a calm day, but seeing the float and accurately throwing feed any distance will be. Fish within your limits, but if you really feel the need to fish at long distance, consider feeder fishing.

Seasons

Fish are cold blooded and like all cold blooded animals their body temperature is regulated by their surroundings. In the cold water of winter a fish's metabolism slows to a crawl. Non native species like common carp can become almost dormant, shoaling together in the warmest part of the lake hanging virtually motionless in the water. Native species are less affected and may feed for short periods in the warmest part of a winters day. They won't need much to eat, not only because their metabolism is so slow, but because the chemical reactions of their digestive process will also be slowed by the cold.

Come the spring, the days get longer and lake water begins to warm and the fish become more active. At first there will be little for the fish to eat, it takes time for plants and insects to grow and appear. Having used all their fat reserves in the winter, there is a period before fish spawn when there is little to eat, but they are actively looking for food. March, April and May can be some of the best months to go fishing, but pick your days.

As spring gives way to summer, more and more people go fishing. I can understand why people like to fish when the weather is fine, but the heat of a summer day is not the best time. Some species quite enjoy the warm weather, rudd for example can be caught on the drop, but on the whole, fishing in the middle of the day can be disappointing. The best time to go fishing in the summer is either early morning, or evening into dusk. I'm really not a morning person, although there was a time many years ago when my eagerness to catch was stronger than my bad mood of a morning, thankfully those days are well and truly past.

At the height of summer I like to set up late, just as others are heading home. As people leave, peace falls over the lake and the fish come on the feed closer in than they have all day. Tench stir the bottom sending up showers of tiny bubbles. Roach and rudd break the surface taking insects and the carp, which have been cruising around the surface all day, drop down to feed. Comfortable in the cool evening temperatures and without the sun in my eyes, I will get a good four hours of blissfully undisturbed fishing.

October brings a change. The days shorten too quickly, and before you know it the clocks are going back. Some days are warm and some dump cold rain into the water. Picking a day to go fishing in the changeable autumnal weather is done at short notice. The fish will have one last push to build fat for the winter, but the fishing can be hit and miss.

Christmas and new year duties discharged, we are back to the short dark days of January and February. Unless there is a warm spell, I restrict myself to river fishing, at least there the fish must feed to maintain their strength to resist the constant flow. As the seasons pass, the best time of day to be by the water changes. Midday to mid afternoon in the winter, moving out to sunrise and sunset in the heat of summer. There are no hard and fast rules dictating which part of the day is best, but seasonal temperatures are a helpful guide. After the seasonal time of day, the weather conditions on that day are the next important factor. Ideally the weather has been stable for two or three days beforehand. A drop in temperature is not as appealing as a rise. Warmer and overcast is usually better than warm and bright. Frosty and bright can be very hard, but stupidly hot, bright summer days are as uncomfortable for the fish as they are for the angler. Cold North or Easterly winds will put the fish down, whereas the opposite is true of warm winds. I accept you may not always have a choice, but avoid extremes of weather if you can.

Float fishing does not discriminate between species. Waggler fishing a single maggot on a size 20 could catch you any fish in the lake, big or small. Sometimes it is possible to weed out certain fish by selecting a spot where they are not found. Or by using different presentations for certain species, rudd on the drop, tench off the bottom are good examples. Frequently though, peg selection is about choosing one with the highest probability of not blanking.

Choose a peg

The broad brushstroke of which part of the day is best to fish, does nothing to help decide which peg. Some waters I have been fishing for decades and I like to think I know them well, others not so much. I look at any recent match results, consult my notes on the place and check the weather to build an opinion, but the final selection has to be made at the lake. At all times of the year, fish will be where they feel most comfortable, or where they know to find food. It is not unreasonable to assume that fish will move from a place of comfort to another to feed. On many occasions a regular pattern of movement is seen, a regular patrol route to all the likely places a fish can find food. An angler who baits a patrolled area, is likely to have periods of activity as the fish come and go. With careful feeding, you may be able to keep the fish in your swim long enough to build a good catch, but much depends on the habits of the species of fish in the lake.

A bed of bulrushes will be an attractive area for the fish and a feature to fish against, but they could indicate a change in depth. Bulrushes rarely grow in water of more than two foot and lilies struggle in water of more than three feet deep. A rough plumbing of the area will be needed to identify contours, slopes, drop-offs, holes and any other relevant feature of the lake bed in front of your peg. On a managed lake, it's not unusual to find a shelf in front of weeds before an increase in depth. Look for an area around 3 or 4 feet deep to begin with.

There will be places rich in food where the fish will naturally spend more time feeding. Different species have their own ecological niche, these holding areas will vary between species, but only if the lake is environmentally diverse. A man made water with a uniform depth, is never going to be as diverse as a water with a deep end. A lake full of weeds will nearly always have a greater abundance of natural food than a heavily managed lake.

Finding the shallow areas and deep holes, noting where the weed beds and islands are, we can build up a map of the lake which will help in finding the fish. There may be more than one place of interest, there could be several places that overlap. Consider how the wind and sun affect the water, give yourself a much clearer idea of which side or corner of the lake to concentrate your search for a peg. Your selected area may contain a popular peg with a worn bank. On the assumption that dozens, even hundreds of anglers have previously selected to fish there, this is probably a good spot. If this popular peg is already occupied, or not suitable for float fishing, then another peg on your chosen bank will have to suffice.

Once you have found a peg for the day, either by careful reasoning, or wishful thinking, the matter of where precisely the fish want to be has to be decided. The swim may have an obvious feature to fish against, in which case there is no point in overthinking, just fish that spot! Otherwise a detailed assessment of the make-up and contours of the lake bed is needed.

Casting around the swim with just a bomb on the line will reveal the make-up of the lake bed. Cast out then slowly pull the bomb free of the mud and feel how much effort is needed to release it. A light pull indicates a firm bottom that the bomb barely sunk into. A harder pull suggests the bomb sunk further into soft mud or silt. Drag the lead along the bottom to feel more of the lake bed. Sometimes a sample of the lake bed will stick to the bomb, a close inspection upon recovery can yield useful information as to the precise make-up of the lake bed. If leaf material comes back with the bomb, a lake bed covered in decaying leaves can be suspected. The amount of leaf litter will depend on the time of year. Understandably, autumn and early winter are the times when the lake contains most leaf litter. As a west, south-westerly wind prevails here in the UK, it's not uncommon for floating leaves and other debris to be blown to the east, south-eastern end of the lake, which eventually sink to the lake bed. It follows that often the south-eastern corner of the lake has either the most fertile area of lake bed, full of natural food like bloodworm, or the lake bed is the most smelly, revolting black sticky mud covered bottom beneath a layer of debris. Deep holes, the foot of ledges and other features may also collect silt creating either of these conditions.

Mature silt is made from very fine particles of material. Bubbles of gas and clouds of muck will be released from silt as fish search for food. These emanations are a sure sign of the presence of fish. Bubbles released by the activities of a feeding fish differ from the natural release of gas caused by the decay of matter on the lake bed. Natural releases of gas usually produce a stream of large bubbles which appear in one place at the surface. Whereas bubbles of gas released by a feeding fish are generally smaller and may appear in a string or as a cloud of tiny bubbles.

Seeing the lake as a whole, narrowing down an area and selecting a peg, plumbing the swim, choosing a spot, finding the "how" by float and presentation are all things that can be arrived at with a little work and observation. Wanting to catch a particular species is usually the best first thought. It will lead you to find the "where" and "how". It will guide you to which rod, strength of line, size of hook and so on. This is why whenever you ask a question of an experienced angler, they will answer you with the question: "what do you want to catch ?".

For many, a day fishing is as much about getting out as it is catching fish. Perhaps the anglers I saw looking up the lake for a few seconds were not experts, but people who just wanted to enjoy a day by the water catching a few fish and to be honest, why not.

Feeding

When I first started fishing, I thought all I had to do was ping out several pouches full of feed and cast over the top. Then I witnessed a natural event which helped me realise I was wrong.

Looking down from the top path as I approached the lake, I could see a large shoal of roach and the odd carp close in to the bank, but what they were doing there. I carried on down to the lower path and walked along to where the fish were. At first I couldn't see what it was that was so interesting, but then I noticed every few minutes a winter moth caterpillar dropped from an overhanging oak tree. All became clear and I learnt a valuable lesson.

The fish were there to feed on this bounty from heaven. Looking up at the tree, I could see many of it's leaves were damaged by dozens of bright green caterpillars. These were winter moth larvae. The fish had gathered under the tree to eat the caterpillars as they fell into the water. It wasn't raining caterpillars, just now and then one would drop from the tree and two or three fish would go for the grub. These fish were in a spot I did not expect to find them, but the constant drip of food attracted and held them in this place. This was a natural event which demonstrated how well even a small amount of food dropping into the water will bring fish to one spot. Regularly feeding a few maggots will have the same effect. Over time fish will discover the maggots entering the water and stay in the swim in the hope of finding more. As more time passes and more maggots drop in, the fish become almost frantic to take advantage of this windfall while it lasts. By regulating the number and frequency of maggots, it is possible for an angler to create competition between the fish in their eagerness to eat a maggot.

At first most of these fish are small. Most waters seem to have a good head of juvenile fish, whether they be roach, perch or some other species, so no surprise they are the first on the scene. In time a better stamp of fish will move in attracted by the commotion. Trickling a few small items of bait may be a rudimentary form of feeding but it is a genuinely effective method as proven by the winter moths I saw.

The most reliable way to proceed is to begin by regularly introducing small amounts of feed to provoke a reaction from the fish. The reaction we want is for them to show an interest and begin feeding on our free offerings. Once one or two fish begin to feed, others will follow. In time they will compete for the food and that's when catching them becomes much easier. The sound of the feed hitting the water is what initially attracts the fish. Water is very efficient at transmitting sound and fish have evolved to take every advantage of this fact, whether it's a warning sound of danger or of dinner. Once they arrive, they watch for the feed falling through the water and intercept it, or follow it down to pick it off the bottom.

With very regular feeding, the fish will begin to anticipate the feed hitting the surface and come up in the water to intercept it sooner. Swirls on the surface, line bites and missed strikes are all indicators that the fish have gone shallower. Most of these will be juvenile roach and rudd, but if there are too many, none of the feed will reach the bottom. This is a problem because the better fish tend to be lower in the water. To ensure the better fish don't lose interest, increase the quantity of feed. The fish at the surface will not be able to intercept all the extra feed, some will get past reaching the better fish giving them a reason to stay.

Fishing on the drop and loose feeding with light, slow sinking baits like maggots and casters is a good way to begin a session. If nothing else it's a sure way of netting a few fish to avoid a blank. If everything goes to plan though, a few better fish will be drawn in. As a rule of thumb, fishing on the bottom is usually better for catching the bigger fish. At some point in the session, prepare for fishing on the bottom by increasing the feed or feeding heavier baits like hemp, corn and or pellets that will sink quickly. Once again, feed sparingly, but be prepared to feed more once the better fish arrive. Drop down on the bottom from time to time, or have a second rod set up with a suitable rig.

The better fish are not always in large shoals. It's not unusual to catch one, two or three, only to find the rest have moved out of the swim. But all is not lost, the better fish will return. They don't forget the spot you are feeding. When their confidence returns, so will they. In between groups of better fish, maintain the little and often feeding regime as before and switch back to the mid water roach, rudd and perch.

Maintain careful control over how much feed is put in. Increasing the quantity of feed can put the fish off or even kill the swim. A common mistake is for anglers to catch a few then assume the swim is full of fish and pile in the feed to hold them. Whenever possible, competition between the fish should be encouraged by rationing the feed. Observation is very much the guide to loose feeding. Watch for signs at the surface, swirls, bubbles and clouds of silt. Look for line bites which indicate the presence of fish, but can also indicate the fish have come up in the water. If you are fishing midwater and your bites dry up, try dropping down onto the bottom to see if the fish are there. Use feed bait you have 100% confidence in. Squats, pinkies, maggots, casters, hemp, pellets and sweetcorn are all baits you can be sure fish will eat. Other baits known to work well are luncheon meat, prawns, pellets and bread in all it's angling guises. To improve the chance of catching in any and all conditions, dispel any doubts in your mind about the bait and use tried and tested bait that definitely work. If you are not catching when there are signs of fish, alter the presentation until you find out what the fish want.

Loose feeding is quite an easy method, but it's not always the best method. Accurately throwing or catapulting loose feed is more difficult the further out you fish. Feed thrown any distance will spread apart in the air requiring the use of more feed to cover the larger area of lake bed. A head wind or blustery wind will have the same effect. In cloudy water, it's better to have something that will disperse into the water which will appeal to the fish's sense of smell and taste than just particles of feed resting on the bottom. The question of attraction, wind, distance, turbidity and for that matter depth, are all answered with a little extra preparation and the use of groundbait.

Groundbait

European match anglers made flavoured groundbaits popular by winning matches in Britain during the last century. Today, flavoured groundbaits are universally used and a great deal of time and effort is put into their development. I feel it is safe to put one's faith in many of the products made by well established companies, but remember the context in which the groundbait is used, in our case float fishing a lake.

In addition to the obvious differences of colour, flavour and feed content, lake groundbaits are further divided into active and passive. Cereal based active varieties break apart quickly and release particles and oils up into the water column which silvers find very appealing. The active ingredient is usually crushed hemp, any groundbait containing hemp will almost certainly be active. Passive groundbaits do not release particles up into the water column. Passive groundbaits usually contain inert ingredients including fishmeal or finely ground pellets which lay on the bottom until disturbed by feeding fish like bream, tench or carp.

On a mixed fishery I prefer a cereal "Lake" type groundbait, most of the manufacturers make a lake groundbait which will contain a mix of flavours designed to attract all the common species. Groundbaits designed to attract a particular species are loaded with flavours known to work on those fish. bream groundbaits usually have brasem, a sweet additive bream and skimmers love, roach groundbaits often have crushed hemp and aniseed, tench frequently respond to a sweetened krill flavoured groundbait. Although these flavours are known to work well with these fish, it does not mean that they will exclude other species from the swim. Using a groundbait designed to attract a particular species will attract other species and there's no getting away from that. There are often novelty flavours on the market and flavours that are popular for a time, but for my money, I'd rather use a bait with a proven track record. That said, I don't suppose anyone makes a bait that puts the fish off !

To prepare groundbait, put some into a bucket, add pond water a little at a time while mixing vigorously. Pass the groundbait through a maggot riddle to break up any lumps and leave it to soak for at least fifteen minutes.

Test the groundbait by squeezing a handful into a ball. If the ball holds together, but easily breaks apart, this can be considered a dry mix which will break up at the surface or soon after. Add more water to create a stiffer mix designed to reach the bottom then break up. Add even more water for a sloppy mix which will create a cloud on hitting the water. Consistency is controlled by the amount of water added to the dry groundbait, at any time you can test a small ball in the margins to see how it behaves.

Use a small separate working bowl to add feed to the prepared groundbait. Most feeds can be added as they are, but absorbent feed such as pellets, may draw some of the moisture from the groundbait making it too dry. This is not so much of a problem with the small amount in the working bowl which is going to be used right away, but if pellets are left in the groundbait for any length of time it's better to dampen them first.

To kick start a swim with groundbait, put a pint of groundbait in the working bowl and add your loose feed of choice. A pint should be enough to make six medium balls. Introduce three balls, then give the fish a few minutes to find and settle over the feed before casting in. Cast beyond your chosen spot and sink the line while pulling the float back to the feed. If the swim is close enough to loose feed over the top, then commence feeding little and often. The noise of loose feed hitting the surface travels at the speed of sound far and wide and is the first tactic in attracting some fish. The groundbait is used to get an amount of loose feed down to the lake bed and at the same time release flavour into the water which the fish will home in on as they get closer. Noise, scent and taste are used to pull fish in, with the expectation of them feeding and most importantly taking the hook bait. Although groundbait is food, the particles are too small to properly feed the fish, it's the maggots, hemp, corn or pellets added to the groundbait that the fish feed on. There are some course groundbaits that do have a high food content, but on the whole they are not suitable for float fishing as they distract the fish from our feed.

Fishing on the drop is a good way to begin, but when you suspect the better fish have arrived, drop down to present a bait on the lake bed. Unlike the endless supply of small fish, bigger fish are generally caught a few at a time. It's not unusual to catch somewhere between two and six better fish before the bites stop. Better fish are often in small groups, you will only catch two or three before they move away. This may not be due to a realisation that some of their fellow are missing, it's just as likely they are displaying their natural tendency to move from place to place in search of food. Either way the important thing to remember is that they will return. Top up the groundbait in the quiet periods to provide something for them to eat when they return. Some anglers recommend balling in while the fish are in the swim to try and keep them there, but I have to say in my experience shelling fish with balls of bait scares them away more often than holds them in place. On the odd occasion when fish are feeding with abandon, balling in over their heads may work, which no doubt accounts for the legendary big catches reported by the angling press. For my money, I would bet on catching a few at a time foregoing the odd red letter day of legend, in return for a steady reliable catch not dependent upon luck.

Eventually the alluring scent of the initial groundbait will dissipate, a decision has to be made as to when to top up. Timing and quantity are the factors that will maintain or kill the swim. The initial two or three balls have a clear purpose, to kick start the swim. The number of balls and quantity of feed loaded into these first balls is judged by the water temperature, which indicates how active the fish are likely to be and by which species you either want or expect to catch. At some point though it will be necessary to boost the swim with additional feed laden groundbait.

A sure sign a swim needs topping up is a reduction in the quality of fish caught. If you've been catching decent roach, but then begin to see smaller roach, consider topping up. If the better fish found on the bottom were 2lb bream who have since disappeared, then top up, but top up with a greater quantity of feed in the groundbait. bream can eat much more than roach, so more feed will be needed to hold them when they return. The use of a working bowl really pays off when topping up. On each top up, a different amount of feed can be added to suit the changing species, size and quantity of fish in the swim. Even if after a time the better fish fail to show, the small fish in the swim will have intercepted much of your loose feed and eaten much of the feed on the bottom. Once again top up, but perhaps with a small amount of feed until something more positive happens.

Interpreting what the fish want begins with reading the conditions on the day. Every day is different. Even if you spend most of your time at a favourite lake, it will be different for every trip. Look at the lake afresh and with an open mind every time. Find your swim and take in all the features around you. Measure the depth, assess the colour of the water and take account of the temperature. Think about what you want to catch, but also what you expect to catch. Is the lake heavily stocked, are there vast numbers of juvenile fish? Consider the rig and the bait best suited to the fish you expect. Remember, float fishing is not very selective, you might be desperate to catch bream, but accept you may have to wade through a number of roach for each bream. This is a normal part of float fishing and although it's rammed down our throats to target a species, in float fishing we can only ever tip the scale in favour of a particular fish.

Put all this visible, measureable, practical information together and use it to create a single impression of how the fish will behave and feed on this particular day. Start feeding the swim with this impression in your mind, feed with the expectation of catching, then see what happens. Remember a float will not move unless something acts upon it. Watch the float, study and interpret it's movements. Decide which are caused by fish and which by the wind or drift, or by your hope filled imagination and tricks of the eye. Watch the water around the float. Look for swirls, bubbles, clouds of silt and all signs of fish. Reel in regularly to inspect the bait, has it been nibbled, is it in good condition? If there are signs of fish in your swim, but they are not taking your bait, don't just sit and hope, change something. Change the depth, change the position of the tell tale, change to a different hook bait, change the hook, change the line, feed more, feed less, change swims; find the answer.

When the fish begin to come, don't assume because you're catching there are lots of fish in the swim that need feeding. There may be lots of fish, but if you over feed them they will simply leave the swim satisfied. Conversely, you could attract too many fish resulting in a free for all which will result in line bites and foul hooked fish. The trick is to introduce enough food for them to settle and keep feeding. Look to control the number of fish and how excited they get, after all's said and done, the most you can ever catch is one a chuck.

Running water

About thirty years ago my local river, the Sussex Ouse, was dredged to control flooding. One result was the creation of a very straight 200 yard section. It's one of the few places I've ever found where the water flows smoothly with very little mixing for quite a distance. Although the flow is very smooth and even from one side to the other, the water in the middle moves slightly quicker than it does close to the banks. After rain the river changes, gone is the smooth flow replaced with the kind of flow you might expect a river to have. Rain increases water volume, causing more water to push down the middle of the river increasing depth and creating a boundary between the fast central flow and the slow water in the margins.

In some places the "crease" will be very easy to see on the surface, there may be a line of bubbles or debris which mark it, in other places it will be more diffuse. The more uneven the river bed with boulders, fallen trees, weed bed and sudden changes in depth, the more uneven the water flow. In some parts the flow can be very disrupted with boils, eddies and back currents mixing the water with no clear run or crease. Most fish prefer the less turbulent flow, which is also better for trotting a float. It makes sense for fish to be in a place that brings food in the flow, but at the same time does not require an excessive expenditure of energy to stay in that place. The slower water close to the bottom, or just outside a crease are two such places. Trotting a float in a straight line between the bank and a crease will almost always see the float misbehave. Water is constantly being pushed out of the way into the sides by the main flow in the middle. To keep the float on a straight course, run it down the crease or fish off the rod tip. Although the float itself may be in the faster water, the hookbait will be in the slower flow near the bottom or near the bank as it slopes down to the bottom. In some instances, the bulk shotting pattern will be the best option to keep the hookbait near the river bed. In a steadier flow where the boundary of the crease is less defined, a strung out pattern is better. It all depends on the flow.

Straight sections are not always the best place to fish. Meanders have more variation in depth, makeup and interest to the fish. Water always flows faster on the outside of a curve. The main flow in a straight section is down the middle, just below the surface in fact. As a river enters a bend, the water tries to continue straight and the centre of flow comes up against the outside bank. The bank forces the water round with the main flow pressed up against it. As the water moves around the curve, it is forced down creating a circulating flow as it moves through the bend.

The faster water continues after the bend, but soon returns to the middle along the next straight. A slack area is formed on the inside after the bend for some distance. Occasionally if the bend is sharp enough, an eddy is formed which over time gouges out a hole in the river bed.

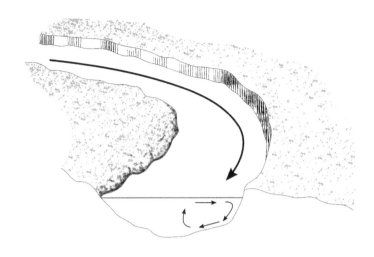

Fig.17 Circulation of water in a bend

Float Selection

A heavy float won't be needed to fish off the rod tip close into the bank. Here the water is slow and smooth with a steady flow allowing the use of a light sensitive setup. Close accurate control can be exercised using a strung out shotting pattern under a traditional lignum stick float. This type of float was originally designed for caster fishing, although they fish maggots, pinkies, hemp, punch bread and other small baits. I cannot recommend a big bait under a lignum stick, but small baits on small hooks work perfectly.

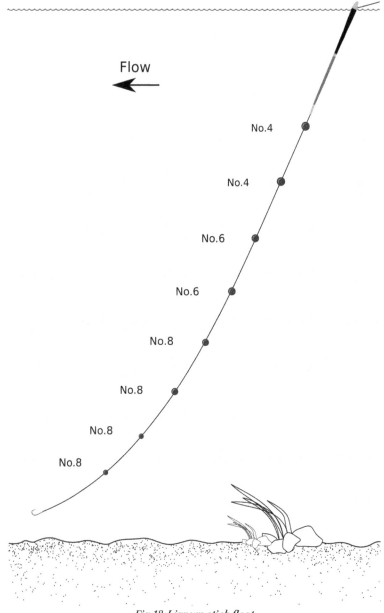

Flow

No.4

No.4

No.6

No.6

No.8

No.8

No.8

No.8

Fig.18 Lignum stick float

Traditional sticks are made of two different materials. The top section is the very buoyant balsa wood. The lower section is made from lignum, a heavy dense wood. The purpose of combining these two materials is to make the bottom half of the float heavy, or at least less buoyant. Unloaded, a traditional stick will partly cock when laid on the water. Small shot equally placed on the line to within 12 inches of the hook, cock and pull the float down to the tip. The proportion of heavy lignum wood to the buoyant balsa top half is critical to create a balance in the float to allow direct contact at all times with the hook bait.

Stick floats are cast downstream of your position with a side or underarm cast. As the rig approaches the water, feather the line so the rig lands softly in a straight line. The instance the rig lands, all the weights being of a similar size and spread down the line, will sink together in unison. At this point the still tight line will hold the float for a second or two as the rig begins to sink. As the rig sinks, the angler controls the pace of the float as it moves downstream. If the float is balanced correctly, the shaft should remain inline with the line below the float. This is the reason why the balance between the two materials in the two halves of the float are so important. If at any time during the descent a fish intercept the hookbait, a bite will be immediately registered by the float. With everything in a taut line from rod tip to hook, one of the most important benefits of a stick float becomes apparent. Striking is instant. With no slack anywhere in the setup, there is no delay or wasted movement of the rod to connect with a fish. I believe this direct connection to the hook is the one aspect of stick float fishing which explains why they are so popular.

After each trot down the swim, adjust the rig's depth until the rig will trot through at half the river's surface speed without snagging. If you plumbed the swim first, you will find the rig is now over depth. The act of slowing the float will cause the hookbait and line below the float to be pushed out ahead. The float will be at an angle to the surface with the main line coming straight back to the rod tip. Under the float, the line and hook link will follow the line of the float down to the bottom. The float will need to be partially held back against the flow at all times to maintain the angle in the line to keep the hook from snagging on the bottom. To control the float, regulate the release of line. Many anglers recommend the use of a centrepin reel. There are plenty of videos on the Internet showing a centrepin adjusted to allow the float to pull line from the spool as needed. I can tell you that unless there is quite a flow and you are using a heavy float, this simply doesn't happen. A light lignum stick does not have enough pull to take line. Whether you have a fixed spool or centrepin, most of the time you will have to manually control the speed of the float.

By controlling how much the float is restrained or released, the depth the bait is presented can be changed. Slowing or halting the float will cause the rig and hookbait to rise in the water. Releasing the float allows the rig to sink down. The ability to change the depth at which the rig fishes as it trots down the swim gives us an extra dimension to explore. It will also allow us to lift the rig over submerged objects or dip into holes. To be able to see bites properly the float should (as much as possible) remain correctly at the surface. A float which is too light for the conditions and flow, will rise up in the water or wobble when held back. The position of the top rubber is important in affecting the float's behaviour. The line should come off the float right at the surface. If the rubber is above or below the surface, the load put on the float when held back will cause it to pivot on the fulcrum which is at the surface. When the line comes off the float on the surface, the float is not adversely affected by holding back.

Striking at bites and mending the line are easier if the line above the float is on the surface. Apply a floatant such as Mucilin or Vaseline to the line for a couple of yards to ensure the line always floats, hold the rest of the line off the surface with the rod tip. My preferred way to control the float down the swim is with the end of the rod. Using a fixed spool reel with the bail arm open, trap the line against the spool with a finger and advance the tip of the rod downstream allowing the float to trot the swim at the desired speed. On some occasions if there is enough flow, I will let line pull from the spool and lightly check it with my finger. Centrepin reels have a fine drag adjuster which can be set to allow the drum to rotate against the pull of the float. As I said earlier, this works best in a fair flow with a big float, light sticks don't usually exert enough pull, in which case paying line out with your fingers might be the best option.

To control the lignum stick properly as soon as it hits the water means casting and feeding downstream of your peg. When fishing within a few yards of the bank, one might feed and cast just a yard or three downstream, with the feed reaching the river bed at maybe four to six yards, depending on the speed and depth of water. It is unreasonable to expect the feed to land in exactly the same spot every time, it will spread down the swim, so expect the taking area to be a line less than a yard wide, but perhaps two or three yards long. Trot your float from above the beginning of the fed area, to a yard or so beyond.

There are no rules regarding how fast you allow the rig to trot, or how often you hold it back, or whether to follow exactly the same line on every trot. What you most definitely should do, is to try different tactics on each pass until you discover what it is the fish want. Once you start catching don't imagine that's it, you've got it sorted, I absolutely promise you the fish will have other ideas. I'm sure you will have to adjust and rediscover the fish several times in a session, this is usual practise and explains why if you watch an experienced float fisherman, he never seems satisfied.

The lignum stick is hard to beat when it comes to presenting a small bait close in, but for fishing on the crease or just beyond in the faster water, a wire stem stick is better. The delicate balance between lignum and balsa is replaced with the stability of a metal stem hanging down beneath the float. Trying to use a lignum stick beyond the reach of the rod and in more turbulent water is not beyond all possibility, it just gets a lot harder. To my mind, no point in struggling with the extra pace and turbulence, just use a float more suited to the conditions.

A wire stem stick float has a slim buoyant body, with a metal rod hanging below it. As with all floats with a wire stem the idea is simple, the weight of the wire stem helps to keep the float upright and stable. Fishing the crease or just beyond, will put the float in more turbulence, which for good presentation requires better control. Fishing beyond the length of the rod means we no longer have the direct control offered when fishing off the tip. Instead, the float needs to be a more independent platform from which to hang our hookbait. All the buoyancy of a wire stem stick is in the top third of the float. The buoyant part is short, partly held vertical by the stem, but also by the split shot pulling the float down. This makes the float less likely to lean, tilt, slant or be pulled over. Turbulent water affects it less, holding back affects it less and mending the line is made easier because of it's stability. There are limits of course, you will need to use the correct weight of float for the depth and or flow. The deeper the river, the heavier the float needed. As a rule of thumb, a loading of one No.4 per foot of depth is a good starting point. The basic shotting pattern is to create a decreasing progression of weight from under the float reducing to very little weight approaching the hook.

Many anglers prefer to use only No.8's which are the biggest shots made from soft lead. These can be moved on the line without damaging it. Grouping two, three or four together, or changing the spacing between individual shots, allows any shotting pattern to be made by sliding the shot along the line. Assembling a rig like this takes time, attaching 20, 30 or more No.8's is a slow business which is better done beforehand.

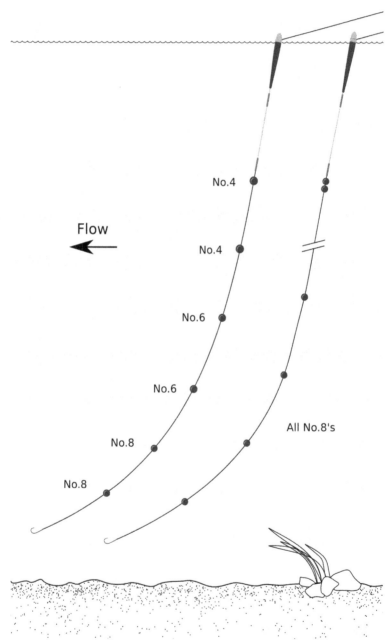

Flow

No.4

No.4

No.6

No.6

No.8

No.8

All No.8's

Fig.19 Wire stem stick rigs

Put preassembled rigs onto a winder, just like a pole angler would. At the river, attach the rig to the main line using loop to loop.

Unlike fishing close in where the flow is relatively even, trotting on the crease or just beyond, puts the float in water that is moving faster at the surface than on the bottom. To offer the hookbait close to the river bed at the same speed as the flow at that depth, the float will need to be held back. Although the float is trotting on a line beyond the reach of the rod, control can be exercised by holding all but the last yard or two of line off the water and by keeping the line behind the float at all times. Hold the rod tip up to keep most of the line clear of the water, and frequently mend the line by lifting it up off the water and placing it back in a line behind the float. Using a floatant on the line above the float makes the task of mending much easier. Control the speed of the trot with the rod tip and the amount of line released.

Holding back hard will cause the hookbait to rise in the water, but probably not as much as with the lignum stick. The greater distance and heavier float make searching high in the water column difficult. In faster, deeper water the fish are more likely to be in the bottom half, if not close to the bottom, searching high in the water may not be needed. Concentrate on presenting the bait at a speed the fish will accept, slow the float and hold back in different spots to find the fish and work out what they want. Sometimes though, what the fish want is not what you expect. On occasions, allowing the float to go with the flow is what the fish want. Even though the hookbait may be moving faster than the layer of water it's in and the float will be in front of the bait, sometimes though it simply works, just remember to strike in a long sweeping action.

From the middle of the river to the far side crease, a bolo, or bolognese, float can handle the distance and flow. Bolo's have an oval body with a carbon stem and easy to see antenna. Some have a body that is deliberately fatter at the top creating a shoulder. The shoulder improves the 'grip' the float has on the water, it holds the float down against the flow when being slowed or held back, allowing better control at a distance or in windy conditions.

The rig is very simple, a bulk of weight in the form of an olivette held in place with No.8's. The olivette is placed halfway or lower, with a dropper shot below. With most of the weight concentrated in the olivette, use a side or underarm cast to ensure the olivette precedes the float in flight. As with all floats attached top and bottom, cast downstream of your position to ensure the line is behind the float as soon as it starts to fish.

The olivette will sink cocking the float quickly, the droppers slowly follow to drop the bait down in a natural way. The distribution of the droppers has quite an effect on how the bait behaves as the float proceeds down the swim. Having a very light shot or no shot at all near the hook will give the most unhindered presentation, but allowing the bait to flap uncontrolled in the current is not desirable. The weight of the dropper shot should be selected to compliment the bait in use. A small light bait will not need as much reigning in by the droppers as a half inch cube of meat or bread flake. A balance between control and natural presentation has to be struck.

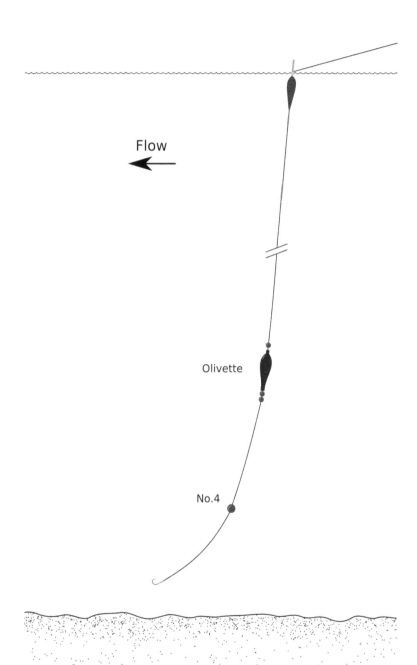

Flow

Olivette

No.4

Fig.20 Bolognese float

Assuming the use of No.8's and smaller as dropper shots, it is an easy task to group some under the olivette, held as a reserve to be slid down as needed. Two or three droppers can be spaced out below the olivette for small baits, but bringing more down in pairs, trio's, quartets or even sextets if needed with larger baits.

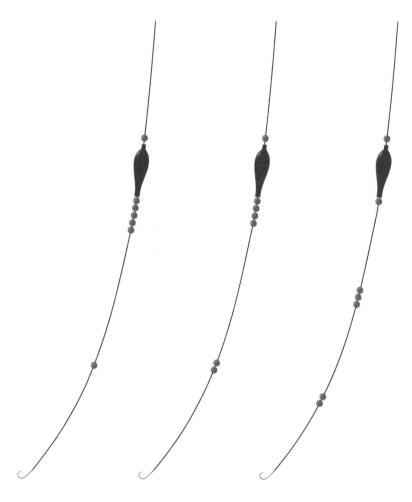

Fig.21 shotting for light, medium and heavy baits

As mentioned when discussing the stick float, the use of No.8's has become common for the ease of moving them without damaging the line. For me, there is another, more practical reason for using small denominations of split shot, which is flexibility. In just a few seconds the rig can be changed from strung out, to progressive, to bulked or anything in between. Instead of thinking about a few larger individual split shot's with a set position or purpose, I prefer to think about weight distribution. That is to say an even spread of weight, a reducing of weight spread or a concentration of weight in one place. Bolo's carry a lot of weight, making it impractical to use only No.8's, but an olivette along with 8 or 10 smaller shot's as droppers is one practical solution.

The further out across the river the swim, the less direct control over the float there is. Every attempt should be made to keep the line behind the float to exercise enough control to keep the float behind the bait. An upstream wind makes this much easier. On occasions though, allowing the float to run through uninterrupted or if the river bed is smooth, allow the bait to drag along the bottom behind the float, slowing the rig down. bream in deep water often respond well to bread flake fished over depth and dragged along the bottom.

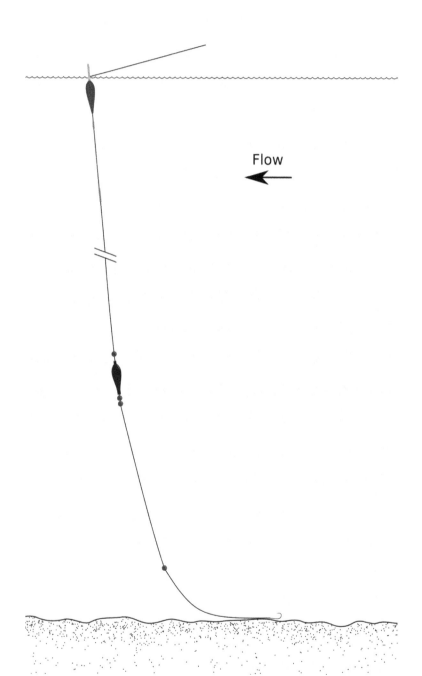

Flow

Fig.22 Over depth dragging bait along the bottom

Controlling and striking at bites when fishing across the river is going to be easier with a long rod. A 15 or 16 foot rod with a progressive action matched with a size 30 or 40 fixed spool reel should do the job. Running the float along the far side crease means the line will have to cross the faster water in the middle. Hold the line up, off the faster water as much as possible, but remember to give yourself room for a sweeping strike to pick up all the line and connect to the fish. Mend the line against the heavy shouldered float gripping the water as often as needed. The float may jerk or momentarily move diagonally, just do your best to keep any unnatural movements to a minimum. The bolo is an excellent float for fishing at a distance, it's weight and long bristle make it easy to cast and see.

The lack of control becomes insurmountable when fishing right across the river against the far bank. A stick or bolo would need to be a long way downstream to have the angle to get behind it. The only way is to use a float that will fish itself and that float is a Waggler. All the very same Wagglers used for still water can be used on a river. The principal of having most of the weight grouped around the base of the float for casting still applies. In stillwater we were most concerned with the float drifting resulting in an unnatural presentation. On a river we are more concerned with the bait moving with the flow as naturally as possible.

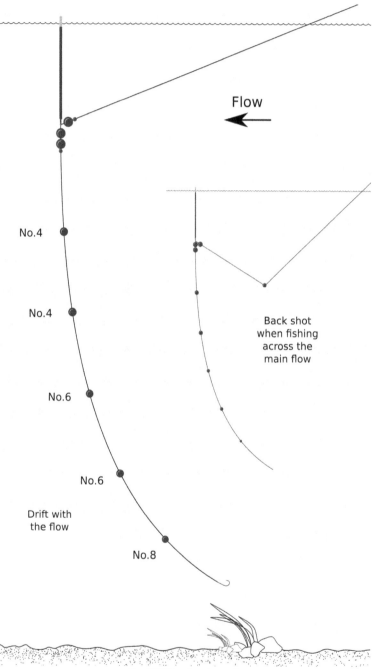

Flow

No.4

No.4

No.6

Back shot
when fishing
across the
main flow

No.6

Drift with
the flow

No.8

Fig.23 Waggler river rig

There are two fundamental ways to trot a wagger down a river. Either letting it go with the flow, or slowing it's progress by allowing the bait to drag along the bottom. On a swim known for midwater fish like roach, dace and chub, allowing the flow to take the float is usually the best presentation. A progressive shotting pattern with either individual shot or grouped No.8's will cock the float immediately, but also allow the bait to sink slowly in the lower half for bites on the drop. On a swim known for bream, fishing over depth dragging the bait slowly along the bottom can be very effective, especially if the water is coloured.

It is good practise to sink the line to combat surface skim when Waggler fishing on still water. There are times when sinking the line on a river is of use, but not trotting down the far side. The faster water in the middle will drag the line into a large bow and at the same time pull the float off line drawing it into the main flow. As with the bolo, hold the line up off the faster water as much as you can. A Waggler can be pulled under if the line is affected by wind or current too much, slightly under shotting the float to allow more buoyancy at the tip. Alternatively, add a small back shot 12 inches above the float to act as a cushion between the line and the float.

Fishing a bend

The river bed on the outside of the bend is usually the deepest part of the meander. The river bed then progressively shallows to the inside of the bend. The faster water on the outside erodes at the bank and river bed creating a deep area scoured out by the force of the water and the actions of small stones and pebbles. Whereas on the inside the slower water deposits fine material creating a smooth, soft river bed.

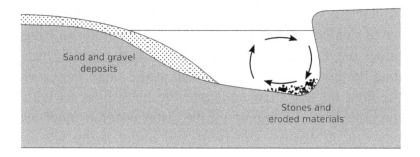

Fig.24 Meander cross section

Fish will only remain in the deep water on the outside when the flow is not too strong. No fish in their right mind will stay in the debris filled turmoil when the river is up. When the flow gets to a certain point, fish will move to somewhere safer out of the turmoil, but they don't usually move far. Generally, most species will stay in an area of river all year round.

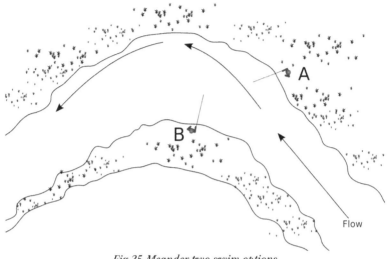

Fig.25 Meander two swim options

Let's imagine there is a choice between two pegs to fish from. The first is on the outside of the bend at point 'A', the second is on the inside at 'B'.

The deepest water and strongest flow are under the feet of an angler fishing from 'A'. Trotting a float around the outside of the bend from point 'A' is the obvious swim to try. In the summer, the water moving on the outside of the bend may be steady and even. It will be possible to fish off the tip, so a lignum stick would be a fine choice. If there has been some rain, the water will be deeper, moving faster, with turbulence and maybe some boiling. A heavier float will be needed to keep the bait in the slower water near the bottom. A bolo could be used, but a wire stem Avon might be a better choice. Fishing so close does not require a float with a long tip like the bolo has. Being able to underarm the rig in reduces the possibility of tangles allowing the use of a wire stem. The stubby top, fat body and wire stem of an

Avon make it very stable. Like the bolo the weight is concentrated below halfway with droppers below to control presentation.

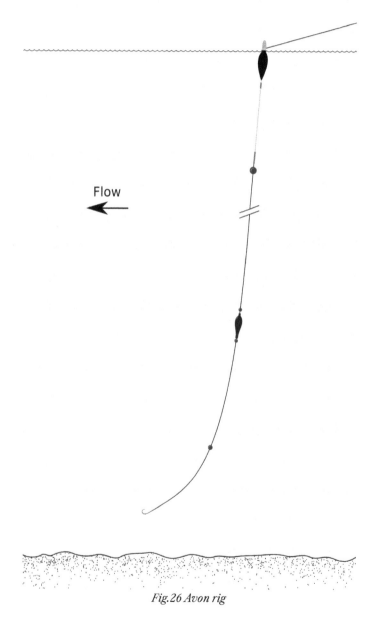

Fig.26 Avon rig

Fishing from point 'B' offers a completely different perspective on the swim. On the inside of the bend, there is no chance of getting behind the float to hold it back or exert any control. Instead the float can be guided around the outside of the bend with point 'B' as the pivot. A Waggler, perhaps with a back shot, would be ideal in reasonable conditions. In a strong flow or poor conditions, a bolo with the bait set to just trip along the bottom would offer a good presentation.

An angler has maximum control when fishing off the rod tip using a light sensitive lignum stick. A wire stem stick takes over when fishing the near side crease. The faster, deeper middle of the river out to the far crease calls for a heavier, easier to "cast and see" float in the form of a bolo. Finally, fishing the far bank where a float that fishes itself is king, a Waggler is used.

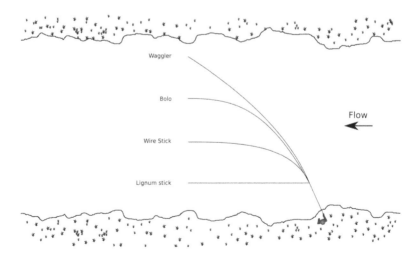

Fig.27 Overhead view of all four floats in our perfect swim.

I started this section describing a lovely stretch of river on a perfect day, going on to float fishing from close in to the far side. Though I have no doubt there are times when these conditions are met, I also have no doubt that these times are few and far between. However, it should be apparent that distance affects how much control we have over a float. Speed of flow and or the depth of water affects the size (weight) of the float. We can also say that shouldered floats "grip" the water better offering a more stable point to mend the line against, but also a shouldered float is less likely to lift up in the water when held back.

The imaginary perfect stretch of river I used to describe the use of different floats was just that, imaginary. However, it served to demonstrate the possibilities and to show what water conditions suit which float. When trotting a swim, we are paying all our attention to a narrow strip of water and river bed below it. Finding a spot to fish may involve looking at the river as a whole, following the flow, working out what is happening under the water and then selecting a good spot. Once settled into a swim though, attention is turned to the strip of water we intend to fish. It's the water conditions within this strip that need to be assessed to be able to pick the best float. No matter how far across or where in the river, how the water flows in the strip dictates the float.

The wind

Wind strength and direction has an effect on river float fishing as it does stillwater. Line control is definitely easier in an upstream wind, it keeps the line behind the float and surface skim helps to slow the float. In a downstream wind the line can accelerate past the float removing all control and creating a loop of slack line. Constant mending of the line is needed to keep it behind the float, but as soon as the line is lifted off the water a downstream wind will get under it, lifting it up, making it difficult to mend.

It's not often the wind blows straight upstream or downstream. It can come from any direction, some directions more helpful than others. I have drawn a guide showing the best and worst wind directions, for trotting a float attached top and bottom. As an example, trotting a lignum stick would be difficult with the wind blowing across the river into your face. This "unhelpful" direction would cause the float to move diagonally towards the near bank. Conversely, a breeze blowing the opposite way, coming from the "helpful" direction will aid in keeping the line behind the float, potentially allowing the use of lighter floats further from the bank.

Trotting in a downstream or unhelpful wind can be made easier by using the Bolo or Avon floats. Both of these floats can carry a good amount of weight and combined with a large buoyant body give something to mend the line against. When the wind is strong though, a Waggler is called for. A Waggler holds the line down in the water away from the wind and surface skim. When fishing directly downstream or fishing slow water, sink the line to get it out of the wind. When fishing across the flow, it can help to add a small back shot 6 to 12 inches above the float, then hold the line off the water against the back shot.

Although it is sensible to use as light a float as possible, using one that is perhaps a little heavy, I would say is preferred on windy days. A No4 shot per foot of water is a good place to start, but in windy, poor conditions or after heavy rain, a No.1 shot per foot may be better. The ultimate test is to see how you feel as the float trots down. If the setup "feels" wrong, then it probably is. It is difficult to describe, but you should still feel comfortable and in control of the float whether it's windy or not.

Choosing the best float to use on the day is completely reliant on river and weather conditions. It is a mistake to decide to go stick float fishing during a dry spell, when the river is so slow that you cannot use one of the sticks best properties, it's ability to search the layers, or decide to trot a big lump of flake along the bottom of a bend when the river is running fast. Every trip you must assess the river, decide where to fish and then decide how. In time you will get to know the river, how it changes with the seasons and when it will run fast or slow. This knowledge is hard won over many seasons, which is why most anglers don't give it up lightly.

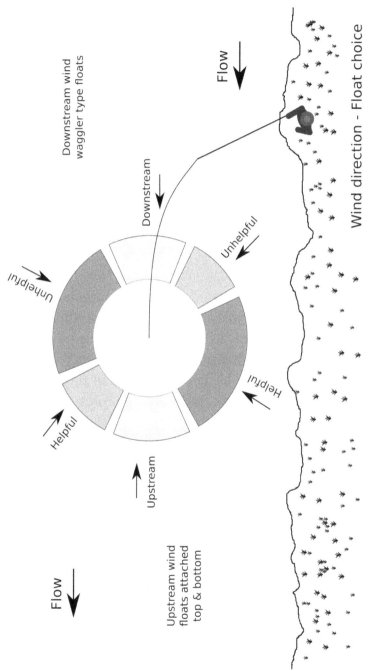

Downstream wind waggler type floats

Flow

Downstream

Unhelpful

Unhelpful

Helpful

Helpful

Upstream

Upstream wind floats attached top & bottom

Flow

Wind direction - Float choice

Fig.28 Helpful and unhelpful wind directions

Finding the fish

For many years I would walk a stretch of river in search of areas I felt were favourable to the fish. In recent years I have adopted an alternative two prong approach by first looking for places I'm sure the fish won't be, then studying the areas left as the most likely places the fish will be. It may seem a waste of time to take note of where the fish aren't, but I find it causes me to take in more of the river allowing me to separate promising sections from which to make my choice. In my opinion, using a process of elimination to discount unfavourable sections, adds to the list of favourable places that warrant closer study.

Few fish like to be tossed around by turbulent water. Swims with boils, swirls and curls on the surface are frequently barron of fish. Strong currents, disturbed water and quick changes in direction can also be discounted. This doesn't necessarily mean there are no fish at all, but I doubt they will be present in any numbers.

Seasonal variations should also be taken into account. The outside of a bend may be a great holding area in the summer with food sinking into the slow deep water. But after the first autumn storm causes dying vegetation, leaves and twigs to enter the river, the quiet deep water becomes a turbulent fast moving storm full of debris which will include gravel and even pebbles. No self respecting fish is going to risk injury for the odd spec of food that passes by at breakneck speed. When the weather is cold and the rivers are up, fish seek shelter, discount all the turbulent areas, study the steady flows, the quiet spots and the deep water.

In the summer, all fish are active, but so are the predators both in the water and from the air. If the weather is very hot you may see fish basking, but usually they hide on bright days in weeds, under trees and in snags. Wearing polarized sunglasses is essential in the game of hide and seek, but if you can see the fish there can be no doubt you've found them.

Many anglers extol the virtues of undercuts, sections of bank that have been undermined by erosion creating a hollow in which the fish can hide. There is no doubt that some undercuts become inhabited in favourable conditions and in low flow, although they may be evicted by strong flow. If the undercut has roots and vegetation growing through it, all the better for the fish, snags within an undercut make the fish feel safer. Tempting a bite can be difficult, timing and the right approach is called for. Fish may venture out in poor light and darkness, so fishing at the right time using a bait that you have faith in is probably the way to go. Don't expect to catch a netfull from an undercut, in most cases we are looking to catch one or two decent fish before moving on. Stret-pegging or laying-on are probably the best float methods, although often ledgering is the very best approach.

I once fashioned a metal rod two feet long that sat at right angles when screwed into a landing net handle. With this I was able to prod and explore the banks of my local rivers in search of undercuts. Despite spending two sessions, covering miles of river, I did not find any. I did find fissures in the bank walls, but no undercuts. The soil in my area will not support the bank over an undercut. As soon as the bank begins to erode, the bank simply slumps into the river, which is why I was unsuccessful with my prodding tool. What it did explain is why in many places there is a step in the river bed. I might not be able to find an undercut to fish, but I know for sure how these steps appear.

Knowing the topography under the water and around the river will be a great help. Take time to thoroughly plumb sections and also determine the nature of the river bed, is it silt, sand, stone, hard or soft. Do at least two surveys, one in the new year after the floods and before new growth in the spring. Take a second in the summer when all the rushes, reeds and weeds can be seen and mapped, between the two a very clear picture can be built. Needless to say this can be done over several visits.

Use all the usual resources to find promising sections on which to concentrate. Select a stretch that has at least a couple of meanders, bankside trees and some variation in width and flow. Spend a day plumbing, inspecting the bank photographing everything of interest. Photos are a valuable resource, with the best will in the world you won't remember everything. Being able to look back on exactly where weed beds were in the summer and having pictures of the banks taken in the winter will show you safe areas to stand and where the fish might be.

Few people can spend as much time as they would like on the bank. So when you are, take time to walk your chosen stretch, observe the changes and notice the fish. Fortunately, watching a float trot downstream puts the angler in an ideal position to glance away at a fish's movements, ripples and bubbles. Even when you are busy fishing, be conscious of the river, proactively take in every piece of information and constantly update your local knowledge.

There are many other features on a river that must be assessed and accounted for when deciding where and how to fish. Obvious things like weed beds, fallen trees and undercut banks are all features to consider, but every river is different and every river is in flux. From one season to the next rivers change, flooding and erosion being the main forces. Unlike a stillwater where changes take time, a river can literally change overnight in one big flood. Regular visits and fishing your favourite stretches is the best way to stay in touch with a river and keep catching.

Feeding

Hope and anticipation are the emotions that often drive us to give hours of our free time in preparation and planning. On the day, after a week at work, walking down to the river is a wonderful feeling. Walking it's banks in search of a good spot, or just dropping into an old favourite, there is something uplifting about getting away from it all for a few hours and catching some fish. Surely few of us go fishing long faced and miserable. Pleasure is taken in tackling-up, plumbing the depths and settling down to a day fishing. With everything just so and as ready as it can be, a good mood and high expectations help cast the float out for a first run downstream. After an enormous amount of time and money spent in preparation, now on the bank it is time to be patient and wait for the fish.

There is a perception that an angler must passively wait, and that it is entirely up to the fish as to whether the angler catches, but this is not true. All anglers who make the most of fishing are busy anglers, in other words, they actively try to catch fish. This does not mean having all the gear, doing the prep and running the float down the swim over and over. It means doing all of that and feeding the swim. Out of everything a float angler does, feeding the fish is by far the most important. If you can lure, entice or beguile the fish into feeding freely, it barely matters how you fish, they become blind to the danger.

Working the fish up into a feeding frenzy in a wild river is more a hope than a certainty. A steady catch of a fish every third cast or every other cast is a more realistic goal, but that does depend on where you are fishing. Consider the size of the river. I know a river which is mostly just 8 yds wide that is on my local club match calendar. Looking back over the results, I can see summer matches are often won by the angler who catches three of four bream. In the winter the matches are won by the best roach angler. Only once can I find a match won by someone with a net of twelve bream, a match fished in June before the bream had split up after spawning. I have walked and fished this river many times, and only ever seen small groups of bream. I don't believe the river suits, or can sustain, large shoals of bream, which explains why matches are usually won with just a few.

A second river I know is twice the width and has more depth. Shoals of over 100 bream are regularly seen in the spring close to the surface enjoying the spring sun. This river has the capacity to sustain many more bream than the smaller. The large catches of bream that make the angling press, are usually caught from major rivers or reservoirs. For some species of fish, the physical size and capacity of a river has a bearing on how many you might hope to catch, which of course has a bearing on how to feed.

Other differences I have noticed are that small rivers seem to have a great many roach of 8 oz and smaller, whereas larger rivers contain a better stamp of fish, on top of vast numbers of 8 oz and smaller. Chub appear to grow to a certain size which is related to the size of the river, although there is always the odd monster in a small river. From these observations we can deduce that piling in the feed on a small river is likely to be a waste, simply because small rivers don't have the population. Big rivers with large populations may well demand a proportionately larger amount of feed to hold the fish long enough to catch a net full.

I think most of us would accept that a big river is going to have more fish and perhaps bigger fish than a small river. It is one of those things we take for granted, but it is a thought that needs to be brought to mind when trying to decide how much bait to take. A small weedy river full of natural food might only need a pint of maggots, not only because of fewer fish, but they already have lots to eat. Whereas a big river with less weed might need a good four times or more bait to be able to feed enough to keep the fish in your swim. The time of year and water temperature also have a big effect, to say nothing of the size and species of fish. Some anglers take this matter very seriously, carrying large amounts of bait to every session. Others take the same amount each time and hope for the best. I try to take what I think I will need. More in the spring, more for a wider river. Less when it's cold, less when I expect the shoals to be small.

Despite the efforts of bait companies, wild river fish respond best to natural baits. Maggots, casters, worms, hemp, tares, corn, meat, bread, are all baits that work well and have worked for many years. In feeding a swim, careful thought and observation are used to measure the response of the fish. The clearest indicator is the number of fish landed, when compared to your expectations. There may be a desire to catch a big weight, but on a small river landing 5 lb of roach would be a good day, 10 lb would be a red letter day. Whereas, 10 lb on a big river may be decidedly average. Just as line, rod and float are selected for the expected fish and conditions, the quantity of the most suitable feed and hook bait are chosen to give us the best chance of catching from a particular river.

Specialisation in one species has become common in anglers and is actively promoted by the angling trade. From a commercial point of view this makes good business sense. It's easier to sell an off the shelf solution and provide facilities where anyone can turn up and catch fish. Although it is possible to target a desired species on a natural venue using environmental and weather conditions, it takes local knowledge and time to know where the fish will be on a given day. Float fishing is not a selective method in itself. A better approach is to try for a particular species, using suitable tackle and bait, but accept that you may have to catch many other common fish before landing your quarry. I have always seen this as beneficial. I prefer to keep busy catching other fish between the ones I am targeting, rather than sitting bored out of my brain waiting for something to happen. As an amateur angler myself, I am not always certain what I am going to catch. I prefer to use tackle that fits the conditions and the size and type of fish I am most likely to catch and feed with a "catch all" frame of mind.

There are two things to look for when adopting a catch all approach. Firstly the water needs to be three to six feet deep, with enough clarity to see two feet down. Fishing at these depths means the swim can be easily fed without needing groundbait. The clarity is important because if the water is too coloured the fish have more trouble picking out feed in the flow or on the drop. The speed of the flow is less important, because there are float fishing techniques for all but the strongest of currents.

To cover as much water as possible, both down the swim and through the water column, the lignum stick float is the best method. A stretch suitable for using a lignum stick has to have a smooth flow close to the bank to be able to fish off the rod tip. This swim should be fed in a way to maximise the advantages of the stick. Loose feed with baits that sink slowly and travel several yards down the swim before touching bottom. Introduce small amounts of maggots or caster and casting into the feed. Control the stick to make the hookbait look as natural as possible.

On landing, feed will begin to sink and be carried downstream, slowly getting closer to the bottom the further away it gets. Midwater fish could take the feed at any depth from just under the surface to just above the river bed. The tight control afforded us by a lignum stick means bites will register no matter when, or how deep the hookbait is. After a while it should become clear how deep the fish are sitting. If the fish are up in the water, bites will be coming on the drop as the float hits the water. If the fish are deeper, the bites will come further down the swim where the loose feed and hookbait meet the fish. Becoming aware of the depth the fish are swimming, allows us to concentrate on that area and optimise the rig to take advantage.

The concept of the further away the fish bite, the deeper the fish are, is an old one, but is valid and easy to understand. A tried and tested technique is to feed the swim little and often, then trot down with the float set shallow. Over time the float is set deeper and deeper and trotted further away until the fish are found. At some point, the fish, the float and the feed will all come together and hey presto, you're fishing.

Loose feeding a slow sinking bait and fishing off the tip with a sensitive stick, is perhaps the best catch-anything that swims method. Small fish can become a problem though, they intercept the bait on every cast as soon as the rig hits the water. This could also mean no bait is reaching the bottom further down the swim. Increase the quantity of feed introduced in the hope at least some is reaching the bottom.

Getting the hook bait past small nuisance fish with a stick can be difficult. The standard shotting pattern is to equally space shoot down the line, moving the shot into pairs will cause the bait to fall through the water a little faster through the small stuff. A single maggot hookbait can be taken by the smallest of fish, a single caster has a much better chance of getting past them. Casters are well known to catch better fish, but it can take time to see results, perseverance is needed. The presence of better fish near the bottom can only be established once a bait can be trotted near the bottom. Every river has stretches known for small fish and other areas where the better stamp of fish are found. These locations can change over time, but it's not unusual to find areas that are persistently populated with a certain size of fish. Doing your research and building up your own local knowledge is the best way to get an overview.

At times when we might reasonably expect the fish to be active, in other words, spring and summer, start with small handfuls of ten, fifteen maggots introduced very regularly. Start trotting and see how the fish respond. On most occasions, small fish will notice the feed first, expect to catch at least a few 2 or 3oz fish. The important thing to do is keep feeding, because small fish activity will eventually attract better fish.

When better fish begin to show, no matter what the species, but usually roach, chub or dace, increase the amount of feed to not only get through the small stuff, but to keep the better fish nearer the bottom interested. At this point start adding some casters to the feed especially if you are seeing better roach. A handful of hemp which is a tried and tested roach attractor can pull the fish in. Hemp seeds sink much quicker than maggots or casters. Throw hemp in separately and further downstream so all baits reach the bottom within the swim. It is very common for the better fish to hang back at the end of the swim. Now and then, allow the float to trot further downstream than usual and hold the float to allow the bait to pause which will often tempt those better fish.

Loose feed can bring fish up in the water, especially if the swim is deep. This has the effect of spreading the fish out, not only along the river, but through the layers. We want to catch the fish where they are, so allowing them to get spread out makes the fishing harder. Getting them to stay on the bottom is much more desirable. A bait dropper can be useful, but I prefer to use groundbait because it has added attraction and flavour.

Mix groundbait in the usual way, but add a little more water to make the balls stick together better to ensure they reach the bottom without leaving a trail down through the water. Separate some of the groundbait into a smaller "working" bowl and use this to add the feed. Don't add feed to all of the groundbait, because once mixed it will be too late to change the quantity. If roach, rudd or skimmers are in the swim, then add small balls of bait to the swim at regular intervals. If bream are in the swim then add three tennis ball sized balls of groundbait laced with feed. Bream really don't like being bombarded when they are feeding, but they are a species that tend to come and go through the day. I find the best plan is to top the swim up between their visits. Catch as many as you can while they are there, feed another three balls before they return. Ball in slightly further downstream of your position. Cast in above and allow the rig to settle then run over the bait. It's not unusual to find fish right at the head of the swim.

Once a feeding pattern is established, continue to employ that pattern and catch fish until something changes. It's highly unlikely there will be a steady flow of fish throughout the day. More commonly, fish will move in and out of your swim causing flurries of activity followed by a quiet spell. Sometime though, a quiet spell may be caused by underfeeding, the fish have lost interest and drifted away. Other times convinced a great number of fish are in the swim, overfeeding results in the fish leaving because they have eaten their fill.

Deciding how much to feed at any given time is perhaps the most difficult skill to acquire. It appears we are entirely at the mercy of the fish, but the choices you make can bring the fish on or kill the swim, so it follows by making the right choices we can entice the fish into feeding and keep them feeding long enough to catch some. Match anglers often watch the angler in the next swim for clues as to what's working. Conversely, having someone in the next swim can also tell you what not to do. Occasionally a matchman will be drawn next to an innovative angler who everyone watches, but these people are few and far between. None of this is of any use to the weekend angler, for us we have to be our own innovators every time we go. In reality, if one in five of your trips is satisfactory, then you are doing well. Everyone has blanks on a river and everyone has red letter days, but by finding the fish, using balanced tackle and feeding correctly, you will have more good, enjoyable days.

Groundbait really comes into it's own when the best swim is deep or some distance across the river. Once the swim is beyond the range of catapulting loose feed, the angler has no choice but to transport feed to the swim in groundbait. Groundbait consistency determines whether the feed is released at the surface or on the bottom. The simplest way to control where the balls of groundbait break up is by using a ready made river groundbait and wetting it by the right amount to get the desired effect. A dry mix will break up more quickly than a damp mix. There are groundbaits designed to be heavy and quick sinking, groundbaits designed for bream are likely to produce a denser mix compared to one designed for roach. The addition of loam, mole hill soil or even small pebbles can be used to sink a stiff ball of groundbait in fast or deep water. When it comes to ready made groundbaits, there is one for every occasion.

Groundbait colour and flavour also play an important part in attracting and keeping fish in your swim. Much like stillwater angling, the colour of groundbait should not contrast the colour of the river bed. Wild fish are exposed to many predators, both from the air and in the water, creating a bed of contrasting groundbait will make them nervous. There are a couple of exceptions. In clear water, black groundbait is usually the best option. There is no doubt that fish feel safer and may even be attracted to a dark cloud of groundbait suspended in the water and laying on the bottom. There will be days throughout the year when all the colour drops out of the water, either because there is little activity, which we might find in the winter, or rivers have slowed and levels dropped in the summer.

The second exception is bread. Liquidised bread, bread crumb also known as bread punch, finely ground bread used as a cloud and mashed bread. roach in particular are very attracted to bread. Other species will turn up, skimmers and rudd perhaps, but bread is irresistible to the roach especially in the winter. The coarse particles of liquidised bread make an excellent slow sinking summer groundbait. Punch crumb I regard as a general purpose groundbait which can be bought infused with aniseed, a flavour much loved by roach. Finely ground stale bread, when mixed with the minimum of water, creates a fine attractive cloud that contains no food value other than your hookbait, usually bread flake, presented within. Despite it's colour, bread is a well known, cheap and easy to obtain bait that has a long and successful track record.

Further thoughts

Balanced tackle

Learning how to find, then correctly feed the fish are the most important abilities a float fisherman can have. These two skills above all else have the biggest effect on how well you catch. While fishing though, it helps to use the correct tools for the job. This may sound obvious, but I see people all the time struggling to get a bite and landing a fish with the wrong equipment. There seems to be a mindset in modern anglers that states, you have failed if you don't land every fish, especially if it's big. I can see why people think like this, as big fish are few and far between, so don't risk losing it when you manage to hook one. Float fishing is far too indiscriminate to target only big fish. Instead a more pragmatic approach is to decide what size and species of fish can be expected in a particular swim on a particular day and use tackle that will improve the odds of catching.

Decide upon an area of lake or river. Narrow it down to a peg, then observe and plumb to find a favourable spot. Assess the swim, look at the water clarity, the depth and casting distance, begin to form a plan of action to begin the session. On a lake a 13 ft rod is usual, unless the water is deep, then a longer rod might be easier. If the water is clear, fishing line is easier for the fish to see, use the thinnest monofilament for the fish expected. I don't ever use fluorocarbon, because despite it's famed invisibility underwater, it's too heavy and stiff for my liking, but it's a personal choice. In clear water I might use a hook link of 12oz to 1½lb and a main line of 2½lb fishing for roach. In the same swim fishing for bream in cloudy water, I might use 2½lb hook link and 3½lb mainline. These line strengths may sound insanely light, but float fishing is a light delicate method that simply works better with light lines.

Playing fish on light lines has two potential problems, the line might break and fish can bump off the hook. Both of these problems are solved by using a rod with the right amount of give. If a rod is too stiff, fish will be able to bounce off the hook against the stiffness of the rod or the rod won't absorb the jerks and lunges of a fighting fish and break the line. Line breakage can be mitigated by a very soft clutch setting on the reel, but this is not an ideal answer. The best option is to use a rod designed for light lines. Any manufacturer who takes the subject of float fishing seriously, will offer two or three stiffnesses of rod in several lengths to suit most any conditions. At the time of writing, I only know of two who offer a good selection of float rods, they are, Drennan Tackle and Cadence Fishing. I find I use my light (lenient) progressive action rods the most, followed by a medium power progressive action float rod. I have no need for a heavy float rod, simply because there are no waters in my area that call for one, it may be different where you are.

Reels are a little easier. Any good quality size 30, front drag reel should be fine. Go to a size 40 with a heavier rod. The spools should be loaded to the top with mono and the clutches set to slip at no more than one third the mainline breaking strain. Balancing the line strength, rod stiffness and the reels drag should make it impossible for a fish to break the line. The rod will absorb the lunges and the reel will let line out if the fish runs. Every fish that is able to make the clutch slip will need to be played out before landing, hauling them in is not an option. Playing a fish with a bit of fight takes skill and patience, but it is also more sporting, after all the fish could get away.

Presentation Theory

For a long time I didn't quite understand what anglers meant by presentation. I would read phrases like "the presentation must be right" and "it's all in the presentation". I understood what the word meant and in the context of fishing it implies how a hookbait is offered to the fish. Over the years I have given the subject of presentation much thought and I offer my own theories in the following.

There seems to be two fundamental categories of presentation. Piquing a fishes curiosity and making the bait look and behave naturally. The first kind of presentation is what carp anglers use. They offer a bait, usually a boilie, which has some property that causes the carp to investigate it. Sometimes it's a bright colour that gets a carp's attention, sometimes the bait is popped up and sometimes the boilie has a strong or interesting flavour. Any one of these or any combination of these, are used to get the carp to mouth the bait, at which time a self hooking rig pricks the carp causing it to bolt. This example of presentation is nothing more than a mouse trap, it entices the fish in and traps it. This kind of presentation is best for specimen hunting where long periods of time can pass between fish, it's of little use to the float fisherman.

The presentation that does interest us is the natural one. A presentation where the bait behaves just like loose feed so the fish can't tell the difference. We want a fish to pick up the hookbait just as it would any loose feed, freely and without suspicion. In float fishing, presentation can mean a number of different things. It could involve how a bait falls through the water, how it looks when resting on the bottom or how it moves in the flow of a river.

Throughout this book I have used diagrams to show shotting patterns and how a rig might look. This is nothing unusual. I'm sure you would have seen many such drawings in the fishing media, in other books and on-line, it is the easiest way to relate the concept or show the basic design of a particular rig. Yet if you watch an experienced float fisherman, you will see him constantly fiddling with the rig, changing the depth and moving the shots around. One might think this expert is trying to find the perfect arrangement for the conditions on that day. I can't speak for others, but this is not why I do it.

I once thought that if I kept experimenting, I would come to a point in the session where I would stumble upon the perfect arrangement of hook, shots and float allowing me to stay with that pattern for the rest of the day. I was searching for the perfect rig for that day. Then I noticed I caught more if I kept altering the rig. At first I thought I had not found the right setup for that day, but then I had a different thought.

I have kept an aquarium in my house for most of my adult life. In that time I have had many different species of tropical fish and one thing I have noticed is no matter what the species, there is always one or two dominant fish. I have had shoals of Barbs, Tetras, Danios as well as bigger Cichlids, loaches and the like, but no matter what the fish there is always a boss, a bully. By watching my tropical fish I know they all have different characters, so it follows coarse fish will too.

Match anglers call the easy to catch carp mug fish, sometimes because they are caught off guard, but sometimes because they never seem to learn and get caught over and over. I suppose this is all to do with the survival of the fittest and perhaps the smartest. Afterall, in the animal kingdom, it's the dominant individual that gets to survive and mate. I can't decide if mug fish are smart or dumb, but what has any of this to do with presentation ?

I believe successful anglers constantly change the presentation to catch fish of different characters present in the swim. Accepting that some fish will be dominant and some yielding to their dominant kin, it follows some fish will bite boldly, whereas others with caution. Older, wiser fish will be harder to fool than carefree juveniles. Finally some fish will prefer to feed off the bottom and others feel safer intercepting their food, so try different depths during a session, under depth, dead depth and over depth. Next time your bites slow down, move some shot, change depth, try a different hook, cast to one side, feed a second spot, move to a different peg, just do something to keep those bites coming.

Feeding Theory

For float fishing I rely on three techniques of feeding, loose feeding, limited initial groundbaiting followed by loose feed over the top and wholly groundbaiting.

1. Loose feeding
   Introducing small, regular amounts of feed by hand or catapult. Judge the fish response and adjust the amount or frequency to suit. Loose feeding is most useful when the wind doesn't blow it all over the place and the water isn't too cloudy, or more than about six feet deep. Take account of the density of the feed to ensure mixed loose offerings land in the same place on the bottom. This applies when considering the rate of flow in a river, but also in throwing the bait out. Light baits cannot be loose fed as far out as a heavier bait. Throw baits of different densities separately. Roach, rudd, skimmers, dace, chub and the odd perch respond to regular loose feeding.

2. Limited groundbaiting
   Two or three balls of groundbait laced with feed are introduced to kick start the swim and get the fish feeding on the bottom. Keep the fish feeding by loose feeding over the top.
   Loose feed will eventually bring the fish up in the water. Tempt them back down to the bottom by topping up with small balls of groundbait. If small balls are not enough, top up with a couple of larger balls, rest the swim to let the fish regain their confidence after such a disturbance, then see if they are back on the bottom. Resume loose feeding with more quantity,

but regularly top up with groundbait to keep them under control. This feeding technique attracts bottom feeding fish like bream and the odd tench as well as all the species attracted to loose feeding.

3. Wholly Groundbait

Use a wholly groundbait approach when fishing at distance, in deep water or in coloured water. An inactive blend is best to keep the fish on the bottom where they will be easier to catch. Mixing groundbait the night before gives it time to soak making it more inert. Start with 3 to 5 balls and see how the fish respond. The amount and type of feed added to the swim can be controlled when forming the balls in the working bowl. A balance in the amount fed and the number of fish has to be found, it's very easy to overfeed the fish as they can eat the groundbait as well as the particles of feed added. Counterintuitively, reduce feed when the fish are feeding to maintain competition and increase feed if they back off. Top up when the action slows to coax the fish into feeding and to attract new fish into the swim.

General feeding tactic

Assess the swim and conditions on the day, whether lake or river. Begin tentatively unless the water is known to respond to positive feeding. Feel you way into feeding the swim. Watch for feeding signals, fish caught and any other signs of activity. Gauge how the fish react and tailor your feeding plan to suit. Remember fish can be very capricious, a bait they craved one day can be rejected the next. Take different baits and experiment if the fishing is slow. Although flavoured groundbait can attract, courser varieties will be eaten adding to the feed volume. Find and feed more than one spot. Use different methods in each to improve your chances.

Groundbait

Much angling advice is subjective and the practise of mixing groundbaits is no different. Match anglers use various combinations to give them a competitive edge and winning mixes are a closely guarded secret. In the world of pleasure angling, most of us just want a simple reliable mix that works. Cereal based groundbaits which attract the sort of fish best suited to float fishing, have been manufactured for decades and are well established and reliable. For us, the practical consideration of consistency, attractiveness and colour are uppermost in our minds.

The cohesion of groundbait dictates how it behaves on entering the water. A damp loose mix will break apart and spread forming a cloud, or a stream of particles through the water column. Ideal when fishing on the drop or in shallow water when the spread on the lake remains tight. Not so good for carrying feed, but excellent if made of fine particles which fish can use as cover in clear water, or create an area of interest to attract fish to an area we are loose feeding. Add more water to the mix and the particles in the groundbait bond more strongly. A wet mix will not break up so readily and reach the bottom in one piece to break up over a few minutes. A sticker wetter mix is more able to carry feed so lends itself to getting feed to the bottom. If a lake is deep, it may be necessary to add an amount of river groundbait, which is heavier and stickier, to lake groundbait to ensure the balls reach the bottom in one piece. A classic example of mixing two types of groundbait to overcome a particular practical problem. Adding yet more water will make our original loose groundbait into a wet slop, once again to create a cloud. This time though a tighter cloud because slop does not explode out as a dry mix does.

River groundbaits are stickier and heavier than lake groundbaits. They are designed to carry feed to the bottom in a current. If a river is deep or fast, the addition of mole hill soil can be used to get the bait down quickly. Just to be clear, mole hill soil is just that, the little mounds of spoil pushed out by moles. Collect and riddle before adding to groundbait.

Many groundbaits are available in two or three shades, usually ranging from light to dark. There are also red and green groundbaits. Red is considered good for tench and green for carp and bream. I have to say that I am not sure fish actually see red or green underwater, they may only see shades of light and dark, either way it's not unusual to lighten or darken a groundbait by mixing two together. In my opinion, anglers like to use a colour they have confidence in. Years of fishing have taught me that groundbait colour is less important than texture and food content. If you are in any doubt, the best advice I can give you is to opt for a darker groundbait, whether it be dark brown, black, or green and black mixed together, I believe a darker groundbait is a safe bet until you establish the best colour for your particular fishery.

If you know the venue and are confident the fish respond well to groundbait, then kick start a swim with balls of groundbait squeezed hard enough to throw and sink to the bottom. Alternatively, to kick start a swim and make the balls last as long as possible, form the initial balls differently to make them breakdown at different rates. One ball, squeeze just enough to throw in and sink to the bottom. Once there it will quickly break up releasing feed and flavour. A second ball squeeze as hard as possible, this will take longer to break down releasing it's contents later than the first. A third ball squeeze as hard as the second, but then wet the outside and squeeze again, this is called "skinning". Depending on how sticky the mix, a skinned ball may take upto 45 minutes to break down. Three balls of groundbait, each releasing it's payload at different intervals permitting perhaps an hour of fishing before topping up with more balls.

Sequence of attraction

I believe there are three ways to attract fish to your swim and they can be thought of as a sequence of attraction drawing the fish closer. First the sound of loose feed splashing down, which instantly informs any fish within earshot of a free meal. As the fish approach, they "smell" flavours dissolved in the water. Enhance this second stage of attraction by adding liquid attractants to water used in mixing groundbait. Popular liquid additives are Brasem, Molasses and CSL. Finally on arriving in the swim, the taste of the fine particles in the groundbait.

Feed two swims

For many pleasure anglers, fishing one swim is quite enough, but why not hedge your bets by feeding and fishing in a second or even a third spot. There are big advantages in having backup swims. They allow us to explore different depths, use different techniques, or loose feed in one and groundbait a second. Having two allows us to rest one swim while catching from the second or alternate between fishing and feeding each swim. If you are fortunate enough to own more than one rod, the possibilities open up still further. Two completely different rigs can be tried, one swim can be close with a second further out, one could be for deep water and one for shallow. Given a choice, I like to open more than one swim, but three is usually my limit.

Intuitive feeding

Accepting that feeding the fish is the most effective means of improving your catch and enjoying your day, the question remains, how on earth is it done. I have already given you a starting point, with practical examples scattered throughout this book, but explaining the "how" in words is difficult. If you were to see me on the bank and ask how, I would reply "I just seem to know how", which is not very helpful, but I'm fishing and would prefer you to just go away.

If you were to stand quietly and watch, you would see me constantly altering the shotting, moving the float and all the other little actions that increase my chances, but these things do not bring fish to me or keep them there, they only allow me to catch as many of them as I can. Looking at my baits you would not see anything out of the ordinary, no secret baits, no experimental flavours, just the usual maggots, casters, dendrobaenas, pellets, corn, bread and so on. So what am I doing that you cannot see ? Put simply, I am using my intuition. I know what you are thinking, that's as useful as saying "I just know"; please let me explain.

Intuition is something we all have to a greater or lesser degree. If you drive a car, then I'm sure you have had the situation where you see a car in a side road and you just know they are about to pull out. But how did you know, what was it about them that warned you ? On the other hand, if when you drive you are the one frequently surprised by what other road users do, then I am sorry to say you are the one pulling out in front of me.

Intuition is acting without the need of conscious thought, reading a situation and reacting to it. Intuition is how some anglers seem too lucky for words. Fortunately it's a skill that can be learnt without too much trouble.

There are only three ingredients needed to make intuition and none of them is hope. I see anglers all the time launch a barrage of groundbait out into the water in the "hope" of catching some fish. A couple of hours later they are wandering around the lake asking me how I do it, to which I reply "I just seem to know how" at which point I "hope" they go away. No, the first ingredient is experience. Sorry, it really is experience. The more often you do something the more you learn about it, especially if you are paying attention. Intuition will not come if you are passive about your fishing, you need to be active, thoughtful and observant.

The second ingredient is expertise. Become proficient at all the skills used in angling. Read as much literature on the subject as you can, both old and new. The Internet can be useful to answer specific questions, but is of little use in gaining expertise. Go fishing as often as you can. Make mistakes, make lots of mistakes, the more the better, because you will learn from them. Accept that no one is born an expert, it will take time. If you tell people you are an expert, almost certainly you are not. When you believe you have much to learn yet are better than most others, then you are an expert.

Once you have experience and expertise, the third ingredient is the catalyst that switches on intuition; immersion.

For intuition to switch on you must be fully involved in what you are doing. I don't mean concentrating so hard on the float that your head aches. I mean completely immersed in everything that's going on around you. See the float, see how it moves, notice any boils or ripples, be aware of the wind and sun, notice a fish that jumps at the other end of the lake. I know it sounds like "holistic, at one with nature" type nonsense, but with enough experience and expertise, immersion happens and intuition is switched on. How long does it take to reach this idyllic state.... Bloody years !

Memorable fishing trips

The free stretch

I remember my first trip to "The free stretch". A one field length of the Adur that in my teenage years the land owner allowed anyone to fish. The chap in the tackle shop pointed to where on my ordnance survey map the stretch was, so I bought half a pint of white maggots in gratitude and planned my trip for the following day.

Back then I could fit most of my tackle in my pockets. The bigger items and lunch I strapped to my bike rack in a plastic box. My Winfield glass fibre float rod I tied to the frame of my bike with coarse hairy string.

The free stretch was about eight miles from home, most of the route through country lanes with high hedges and blind bends. As I rode I conjured up images in my mind of how the river would look. I wished for a steady flow with a nice flat bank and pretty rushes in clumps along the margins. I will tackle up and run my float down the flow catching fish almost every cast. Perhaps later in the week I could come back and use up the rest of my half pint of maggots.

I freewheeled down the last hill leading to the river and as I got close I could hear water rushing. Arriving on the bridge I found there was a weir a few yards upstream and the water was pouring over it. Looking further, I could see quite a bit of weed in the river. Not quite as I imagined. Anyway, I secured my bike to a cement fence post and climbed through the fence and made my way upstream.

I was gutted, the river was nothing like I expected. It was quite narrow, full of weeds with very little flow. How am I going to fish this I thought, I couldn't even see a weed free area big enough to drop a line. There was tall grass along the bank which clearly had not been walked through this year and it was the summer holidays !

I kept walking, further and further from my much loved transport hoping it would be safe left alone. Then finally after several hundred yards, I found a small opening in the weed cover just three yards long out in the middle. The water was completely flat and looked as black as ink. In reality it was crystal clear, but shaded from the sun. I could see plant stems disappearing into the depths although the bottom was hidden. This was the first spot even remotely fishable, so I settled down in the long grass and made myself comfortable.

I had two floats in my pocket, an odd looking Waggler and a grayling float. I knew enough to know this was not a swim for the grayling, it had to be the odd looking Waggler. I trapped it on the line with a couple of lead shots and added one down the line which cocked the float leaving half an inch of the tip showing. I wasn't sure if this was right. Unlike other floats I had seen in the shops, this Waggler was painted orange from the tip, all the way down the cane stem and halfway down the cork body. I had imagined that floats had to settle right on the boundary of the orange paint, but with this float that did not make sense. What the heck I thought, I'll just fish it with the tip showing and never mind how far down the orange paint goes.

It soon became apparent that although the surface was clear of weed, the bottom definitely wasn't, it was covered in eelgrass. My plan to let the bait trip along the bottom was out of the window, I had no choice but to suspend the bait midwater and hope for the best. I was quite despondent. Everything I had hoped and imagined turned out to be wrong, I really did not expect to catch anything, but then the float just vanished. I was completely taken by surprise, it took a second or two to sink in; a bite! I struck and connected, I could not believe it, a fish.

I wanted to catch another. I did the same as before, I cast to the same spot using the only bait I had, but this time nothing. A scenario many of us have seen, but what to do? I decided to fish a little deeper on the assumption the fish were in the eelgrass. I moved the float six inches further up the line, I was now fishing at about 3½ feet. I also threw in some free offerings, not wanting to use all my maggots in one trip, I wasted just a few, I thought they might bring the fish out of the eelgrass.

I found the float was still able to move downstream, even though the bait was brushing through the eelgrass. The float might dip or hesitate a little, but more often than not it would slowly make it's way down the three yard gap in the weeds that was my swim. It worked, more roach took my bait. By the time I had run out of maggots I had caught six roach from 8oz to a pound. Not much you might think, but I was overjoyed. I had come to a river I had never seen, to a river that looked hopeless when I arrived, but had caught fish from, because I had worked it out, all on my own.

Back then I had one small book on fishing, there was no Internet, none of my family fished and unless you were a match angler, the local tackle shop was politely dismissive. Yet I had learned the most important lesson I could learn, which is don't make assumptions, work it out when you get there.

I didn't know it at the time, but how I fished this weedy swim was spot on. The roach were indeed in the eelgrass, as well as in the weeds around my swim. Feeding little and often, even if it was to make the maggots last, was the right thing to do in a water rich in natural food. The Waggler setup was correct in allowing the bait to drift through the eelgrass with all the split shot up the line out of the way. The one thing I didn't know at the time was that my odd float was in fact designed for the lift method, I should have used a straight insert Waggler.

Winter Roach Fishing

Given a choice, I prefer to fish for river roach in the winter, they are one of the few species that can be relied upon to feed. On those occasions when the river is in flood, I retreat to a local pond that has a good head of roach. The pond is a little over an acre in size with two islands. The top island has a moat of shaded shallow water around it, in which carp spend hot summer days mooching. The margin of the second island is a popular place to catch tench up to 6lb in the early spring mornings. In the cold months, roach can be found shoaling in the deep water beyond the second island. Here the water bottoms out at twelve feet. Even with a fifteen foot rod it's awkward to fish a fixed Waggler.

Fortunately, the roach are not found hugging the bottom, no matter how cold the weather gets. They prefer to find a warm upper layer to wait for spring.

Although they are fairly inactive, they are not averse to taking some free offering in the form of white maggots.

Emulating the free falling grubs by fishing on the drop through the shoal, often produces a steady stream of roach of perhaps 12oz. I use a fine wire size 22 hook, tied to a 12oz hook link, which is in turn attached to the 2lb main line with a figure-of-eight knot. The float is a canal grey. Canal grey's have a very streamlined body at the bottom, merging into a slimmer stem and tip. As the name suggests, this float was originally designed for use on canals. It is made from a single piece of balsa wood, carefully turned to form it's beautiful lines. It is a very light float ranging from 3 x No.4's to 3BB's and is designed with shy biting canal roach in mind.

In the summer, such a fine float and tackle would be out of the question on this pond. But when it's cold, the roach are the only fish who might show an interest, little chance of a tench smashing me up.

Despite the fact I know the roach will be in twelve feet of water, I don't take my long rod. Over the years, I have found the fish much shallower, sometimes as little as a yard below the surface. My light thirteen foot rod is perfect when combined with the light tackle.

Have you noticed that maggots fall through the water sideways. They don't dive head first, they slowly flutter down taking five or six seconds to fall twelve inches. If I were to hook a maggot in the usual way, through the fluffy end, it will fall through the water quite differently from the free offerings. To try to make my hook bait fall naturally, I hook my maggots through the side, which is possible with a fine wire barbless 22. Although a maggot hooked through the end will catch fish, I like the smug feeling I get when I think I am outwitting the fish.

All I need to do now is find the "taking depth". Experience has taught me, over several winters, that the fish could be shoaled anywhere from a couple of feet to around nine feet deep. The only way to know for sure is to fish for them.

To get the fish feeding, I ping out a very few maggots at a regular interval. I like to use a small catapult that has a firm plastic cup to fire two to four maggots every thirty seconds, to create a constant light shower of grubs that I hope the fish will begin to accept.

After ten minutes I will make my first cast. The rig is an ordinary slow sinking rig to fish on the drop, the only difference being, it is set to half depth. Watching the float carefully, I allow time for the rig to sink. If I get a bite before the float has fully cocked or sooner than I expect, I take that to mean the fish are shallower than half depth. If on the other hand I don't get a bite until the bait has dropped fully half depth, then I assume the fish are deeper. If I don't get a bite at all after a minute or so after the bait has fully sunk, I will reel in and try again.

During the day I expect the fish to change depth. If weather conditions change, or they come up in the water to intercept the maggots sooner, I will adjust the rig to keep it fishing as best I can. Constant feeding and constantly interpreting the float's indications, along with representing the bait, usually result in a reasonable catch. I don't expect to empty the place, but I do try to at least be satisfied.

Fig.29 Canal Grey fished on the drop rig

Tench

If I want to catch some tench, I usually go to a tench lake operated by my local fishing club. It's a place I know well having fished there many times before. There are reeds either side of the peg nearest the entrance, a peg I know does well in matches. A work party has recently removed some of the reeds exposing more of the shelf that goes all around the lake. Tench like weed beds and this weed bed casts a shadow on the water past midday. This matters because tench move to deeper water in bright sun, but in this swim they will stay longer up on the shelf. I plumb both the shelf and at the bottom of the drop-off. As expected, the water is at maximum depth after some recent rain.

The biggest fish I expect to catch is 4lb. I am safe to use 3½lb main line with 2½lb hook link to a size 16. I can fish close to the reeds so long as I use a low sideways strike that is continued into steady pressure, I can then immediately pull the fish away from the reeds before they have time to think.

I start by fishing the shelf just in front of the reeds. It's a calm day, the water is about 2 ft deep, my spot is maybe 3 yards away. I want to detect lift and dip bites, so I opt for a small loaded insert Waggler. Most of the shotting placed around the float with a single No.6 tell tale, presented 4 inches over depth with the tell tale close to the lake bed.

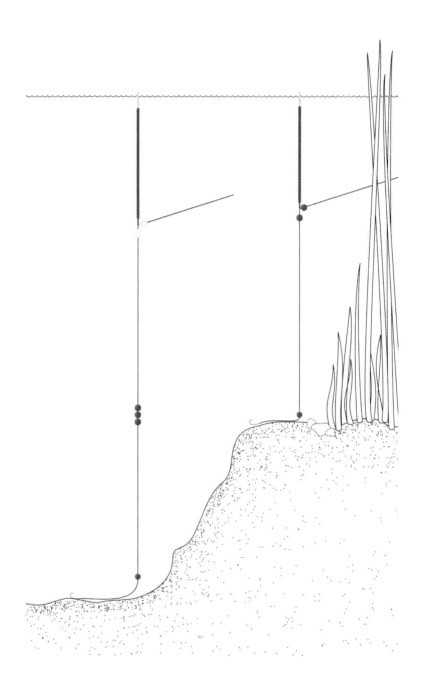

Fig.30 Shelf setup

If the tench drop down into the deeper water later in the day, I can go up one size in float and move the shot down to form a bulk at a little below half depth. If I were to fish from the afternoon into the evening, I would start in the deep water and move to the shelf later.

Fishing so close does not require the use of groundbait, I can easily throw the feed in by hand. I have learnt a combination of hemp, casters, corn and a few cubes of meat serve well to attract the tench. I don't use small baits on the hook, there are simply too many roach. On this particular day though, it was very noticeable that the tench could only be caught on meat. Now that's not to say I had most of my fish on meat, I am saying I had all my tench on meat, they would not touch anything else. On the day I accepted their apparent craving and caught a pleasing number of fish. Later thinking about it and looking into how others had caught, it became apparent that they were partial to soft baits. I wonder if a hard bait is rejected as a pebble or detritus on the lake bed, but expander pellets, meat, prawn and other soft baits were being taken. I had always imagined that taste and colour was a factor, but now I believe, with tench at least, firmness plays a part.

Laying on for Perch

One of my local club lakes, has a good head of decent perch of up to 4lb. In the summer it is difficult to target just the perch, because of the carp. In the winter though, the carp virtually stop feeding, and more importantly, congregate at one end of the lake. The perch are spread out around the margins, they like to be in the dead weed beds, or under overhanging shrubs and hiding under the fishing platforms.

Without getting too close to the carp's winter gathering, I move from swim to swim trying all the promising spots. This is where laying on pays, it is the perfect method for fishing the winter margins.

The rig is very simple, a straight Waggler attached at the bottom end, held in position by either float stops or small shot. Don't use loaded Waggler's because all the weight needs to be on the line. Below the float, a string of three or four shots is squeezed onto the line eight inches from the hook. Don't bulk the shot together, but string them out over four to six inches. Use the right amount of shot to cock the float correctly.

Set the depth so that all the shots are laying on the bottom, with an additional foot of line to the float. Cast out and expect the float to lay flat on the surface. Place your rod in rests and tighten down until the float cocks.

Always cast out under arm to ensure the weights precede the float. This will allow you to cast very tightly to banks, snags and the cover perch love. No need to sink the line as you would when Waggler fishing, because as you tighten down to the float, the line will be pulled straight. Don't worry about small changes in depth, or casting on top of dead weeds or debris, just tighten down to cock the float.

With the float balanced between the rod and the shot on the bottom, any movement will be immediately reported by the float. A bite can register as a lift, dip or a jiggle, but with the shot anchoring everything, when the float does move it has to be a fish. If you are missing bites, then move the shot further up the line away from the hook, this gives the fish more time and room to take the bait. Essentially the longer the hook length, the more confidence is given to the fish. Use shorter hook lengths when the fish are feeding strongly.

I could use any of the tried and tested perch baits, but I prefer prawns because they are bright, smelly, easy to use and the perch love them. Moving from swim to swim, I will throw in a few chopped up prawns as feed, with a whole prawn on a size 10 hook. I'm not sure if it makes a great difference, but I like to use a chrome hook with prawns. Chrome hooks, I think, don't look as obvious against the pink of a prawn as a bronze hook.

I cast into any likely spots, if I catch a perch, I expect to land one or two more before moving on. I don't stay in each swim for long, 15 to 20 minutes, if the perch are there and feeding, I can be sure of catching.

Wind direction and conditions may change as I move around the lake, but laying on is not affected by wind or drift. If the float should become difficult to see in choppy water, I just leave the float a little higher in the water when tightening down.

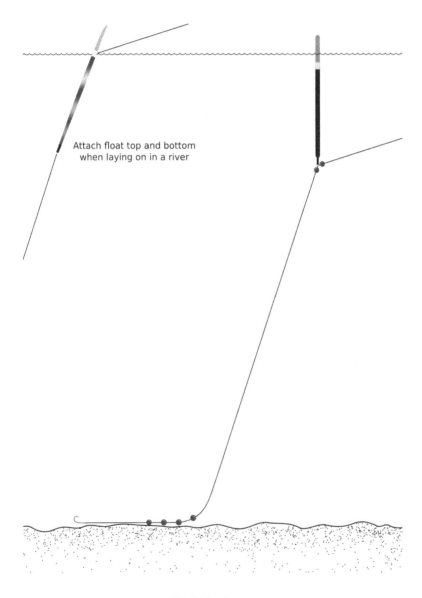

Attach float top and bottom
when laying on in a river

Fig.31 Laying on

Bream on the Ouse

It's easy to get preoccupied to the point of distraction with one aspect of fishing. I fell into this trap a few years ago when trying to increase the number of bream I was catching from a tidal stretch of the Sussex Ouse. I had some success on the swim feeder with breadcrumb groundbait and coarse pellets, but could not catch any on the float. I knew the feeder worked well on an outgoing tide in the deeper areas. I found I could catch roach on the stick or Waggler depending on conditions, which led me to think I needed a different bait.

In a dry spell with a spring tide, the river can be 15, 18 feet deep in the places I caught bream on the feeder. To get feed to the river bed I had to use groundbait. For three seasons I tried different flavours of groundbait in the hope it would attract and hold the bream long enough to catch a few. I tried balling in just as the tide turned to ensure I knew exactly where the bait was on the river bed. I tried different feeds in the groundbait, different amounts of bait and different feeding patterns, but none of my efforts resulted in a satisfying day.

Eventually I stumbled into the solution on a day when I fished between the tides. Although I knew the outgoing tide to be a good time to fish, I'm not always free to go at those times. On this occasion the tides did not suit me, so I thought I would have a break from the bream and just have a "catch anything" day. I decided to fish on the inside of a long sweeping bend, a place I knew to be shallow on my side, deepening down to 10 or 12 feet on the far side.

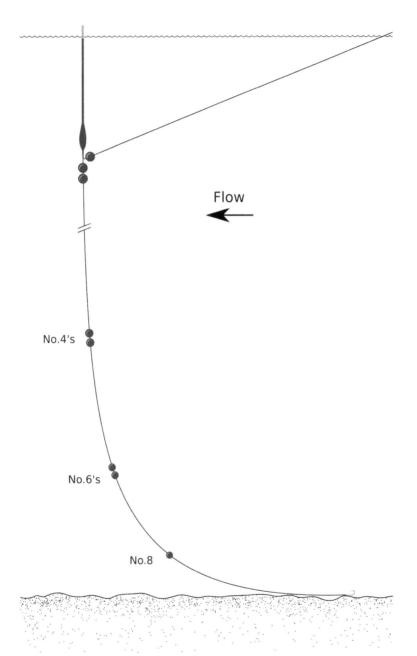

Flow

No.4's

No.6's

No.8

Fig.32 Reverse trotting

The day was warm, but overcast with a downstream breeze. The water was quite coloured with a depth of about five feet. The breeze made it difficult to use a float attached top and bottom, so I used a Waggler. For bait I had liquidised two white loaves (no crust) keeping a few slices for the hook. I began by introducing a small ball of tightly squeezed liquidised bread with flake on a size 14. The wind was making the surface quite choppy and even though I was using a Waggler, it was being pushed too fast down the swim.

Changing to a bodied Waggler, I controlled its progress by allowing the flake to drag the river bed, a technique known as reverse trotting. Not a problem on the inside of this bend because erosion had deposited a layer of fine particles making a smooth even river bed. The float now behaved itself, progressing down the swim in a sedate manner. Continuing to feed small balls of liquidised bread, I began to see signs of life. The first proper bite saw the float dip and sail away just under the surface. It was a bream. As the session went on I saw several bite that sailed away, but I only connected with six of them altogether. Although not a vast number by any means, it was better than I had been doing and only bettered by the feeder.

Clearly I have more work to do before I have a satisfying day fishing for the bream, but this trip is special to me because it removed my blinkered approach in trying to find the perfect bait. It wasn't the bait so much as fishing in the right place at the right time. Although a static bait fished on a feeder worked well as the tide went out, my bream fishing was better between tides with a slow moving bait. I still need to practise this approach, but I feel as if I'm getting somewhere now. Hopefully I will soon have an enjoyable, satisfying day bream fishing on the Sussex Ouse.

Lightning Source UK Ltd.
Milton Keynes UK
UKHW022153150922
408935UK00004B/406